THE HIDDEN WEST

THE HIDDEN WEST

Journeys in the American Outback

ROB SCHULTHEIS

Introduction by Stephen J. Bodio

LYONS & BURFORD, PUBLISHERS

Printed in the United States of America

10 9 8 7 6 5 4 3 2 1

Portions of this book appeared previously, in different form, in
Mother Jones, Outside Magazine, *Mountain Gazette, Playboy Germany,*
and *Rocky Mountain.*

Library of Congress Cataloging-in-Publication Data

Schultheis, Rob.
    The hidden West : journeys in the American outback / Rob Schultheis.
        p.   cm.
    Originally published: New York : Random House, 1978.
    ISBN 1-55821-434-8 (pbk.)
    1. West (U.S.)—Description and travel.   2. Schultheis, Rob—Journeys—
West (U.S.) 3. Natural history—West (U.S.) 4. West (U.S.)—History, Local.
I. Title.
F595.2.S38   1996
917.8—dc20   95-40005
                                                          CIP

This is a Wilder Places book. All Wilder Places books are
selected and introduced by Stephen J. Bodio.

To Alexandra

Of all the many striking statements made by de Selby, I do not think that any of them can rival his assertion that "a journey is an hallucination."

—FLANN O'BRIEN,
The Third Policeman

CONTENTS

INTRODUCTION

EVERY YEAR, IN JUNE, I GO TO A SMALL COLLEGE in a northern
Vermont town to teach a course in nature writing.
Founded almost ten years ago by novelist E. Annie Proulx,
Wildbranch Writing Workshop has been dedicated from
the first to the idea that nature writing, "outdoor" writing,
writing "with trees in it," to use the phrase of the editor
who first rejected *A River Runs Through It*, is not a minor
subgenre but a stream of literature with subjects and atti-
tudes that are vital, even essential, to a healthy understanding of our world.

In our first year, Annie may have known what she was
doing, but I did not. I was a fairly well published writer, but
I lacked a degree and had never attended, never mind
taught, a writer's workshop. I thought my background was
erratic, to say the least. I had almost become a biologist,
but then I switched to writing; I was a poor Eastern ethnic
kid with a fancy New England almost-education who had
lived for more than ten years in a back-country dirt-road
western town with neighbors of Spanish, Indian, and ranch
descent. My only qualifications were, to misquote Tom
McGuane, that I had read like a son-of-a-bitch. I had read
everything from classic novels to field guides; and I be-
lieved John Updike's elegant borrowing—that a writer was
a reader moved to emulation.

These principles, and my attachment to the land of the
West, became my tools for teaching. From my first terrified days, when I talked incessantly while fearing I had
nothing to say, I heard myself saying three things: that
writers had to read; that their love of reading had made
them want to write; and that *nature* writing was a broad
category with only one necessary component—it had to be
rooted, deeply, in real places where humans come into intimate

contact with the land. Nature books had to have trees (cacti, bears, hawks, the wind, sandstone buttes, rain forests, buffalo bones, algae, horses, "how the weather was") in them.

As my fear of teaching receded, I found I held some strong intuitive beliefs about what good "nature" writing brought to literature. Too often the genre was legitimately dismissed by serious writers as either mere polemics or, worse, vaporous internal monologues on what nature means to *me* (emphasis on "me"), the kind of stuff often lumped under the awful neologism "journaling." To claim that nature writing is somehow "spiritual" when it doesn't move the spirit of the reader seems to me a kind of self-indulgent arrogance.

I suspected that there might be another path entirely for writing about the natural world, one that could enrich all literature. The ideal nature writing could be descriptive or narrative, about or agonized by hunting, a travel book, even a book of intimate revelations about ants. But it would embody its ideas in things, in true observations of the real, in intimate, gritty knowledge. Its best practitioners would know animals, plants, rocks; their smells, sounds, tastes, and feel; Hemingway's "weather." These authors would know history, and not be content with only their personal reactions. If the writer knew and lived all these principles, he or she could write polemic or scientific material, comedy, or poetry; all would succeed in moving the reader; all would help us in our endless task of reconciliation with the world. Such ideas may seem primitive, but they remain the base of all effective writing.

I learned from Annie to push my students to write in class, not just in their off-time; to handle short assignments with vivid writing, evoking favorite landscapes, putting real animals and people into them. I searched for writers and passages that would inspire emulation. I introduced my students to essays by Annie Dillard, descriptions of tarpon fishing by Tom McGuane, poems by Ted Hughes. And I brought them passages from Rob Schultheis' *The Hidden West*.

On the first day of class I now read them the passage that begins on page 19 of this book: "If the mysteries of the Great Plains have a heartland, it is the Sand Hills of Nebraska." Schultheis introduces the area with a disconcerting image (one with a structure I suspect he "stole" from Churchill)—the grassy hills are a desert, a hidden one, with more secrets hidden inside them: "A sea inside a desert wrapped in green prairie." He brings you, the reader, into the scene in an intimate, active way, with vivid language that owes nothing to the piling up of descriptive words that students often think characterizes "fine" writing: ". . . dig. Beneath the brittle grass and the thin smoke of soil you hit sand: you are standing in a sea of dunes."

After setting the scene, he gives us a character, Martha Schaller, who was born there of a settler family. I don't know what kind of person the reader would first imagine, but Martha "was six feet tall and weighed about a hundred pounds, still wore the Levi jacket she had gotten for her thirteenth birthday, smoked little black cigars and had been a model in Paris. Her childhood had been a honky-tonk fairy tale." He sets her family in the ghost-ridden landscape:

> Once as she rode home at winter dusk in a swirling Great Plains blizzard, her horse spooked and she looked up and saw (she said) an enormous white wolf, three feet high at the shoulder, leap the barbed-wire fence and race away across the white prairie. There was also an eroded sandstone bluff back in the hills, and when you crawled in with a flashlight you found yourself in a vault that went as high as fifty feet in places. And there were bats: tens of thousands of the ruby-eyed little leather devils hanging upside down.

The "story," all of three pages long, ends in tragedy. Martha's father and his pal blow up the bat cave in a spasm of unnecessary fear of rabies. The Ogallala Aquifer, the hidden sea, begins to dry up. Martha returns to find her father drunk at his desk.

> It's all over, he told her. Sand Hill's cattle ranching's dead. We've got maybe thirty years left, and then the whole business is going to dry up and blow away; from Denver to the hundredth meridian, this country's gonna look like Afghanistan. The dirt farmer and the rancher's gonna be as fifty million buffalo, as dead as Crazy Horse, as rare as a set of jackalope antlers. Ed Weicker and I and every other rancher in this county should have crawled in that cave with the goddamn bats and dynamited the door down from the inside.

I look at my students, as hushed and moved by this set of characters in a landscape, this piece of nature writing, as by any short story or tragic play. And I say, "Go thou and do likewise: write me a piece of landscape that means that much to you. You have ten minutes." And I walk out the door.

I'm not surprised that I haven't quite gotten a *Hidden West* out of my students. But what I do get is consistently amazing, even to its writers. Schultheis suddenly gives them a chunk of landscape, with its biology and blood history, its enigmas and real, hard people; landscape "with the hair on," as Ed Abbey liked to say. It challenges my students to emulation because it is as fine in all ways as nature writing—as *writing*—can be.

The Hidden West came out in 1982 when I was a new Westerner myself. It became a guidebook of sorts into a West that was neither overpromoted scenery nor romantically pristine Eden. Schultheis' West was full of rocks and ghosts, animals and stories and strange people. Schultheis didn't sing about Yellowstone or Santa Fe; his tales were of back country, the harsh badlands that tourists never even heard about. He knew the Sand Hills of Nebraska, deep canyons that drain off the Colorado Plateau in to the San Juan River, Aldo Leopold's lost Colorado Delta, the Tarahumara's Copper Canyon. He knew that the real places, where you can approach the mysteries of a region or have a profane conversation with its inhabitants, are more often than not "hidden." Schultheis knew his science and history and did not give in to facile, neo–native-American mysticism. He had a hard-rock sense of humor. And yet (although he told stories that would make you laugh) he also knew ones that would make the hairs on the back of your neck stand on end.

Maybe another example would help. Schultheis is describing Dinetah, the Navajo country:

> The first time I went down to the Navajo reservation, driving south from Cortez, Colorado, the country struck me with the force of a foreign land: Mongolia during the reign of the Khans or eighteenth-century Afghanistan, perhaps. The men looked like Central Asian cowboys (later, in Tibetan refugee camps in India, I would see the same faces): flat, cuprous, epicanthic faces, many with long hair topped by incongruous felt Stetsons. . . . Driving south to Shiprock and west to Kayenta that first day on the reservation, I found I had entered a whole other cognitive universe; everything was different. Vast deserts of sage swept away to distant surreal mountains. An old Buddha-faced man walked away across the dunes, driving a herd of goats before him. Turquoise pickup trucks rolled down the endless highways. . . . In a café near Teec Nos Pos I ate something called a Navajo taco: ground beef, chili sauce, onions and cheese, on a heavy slab of Navajo fry bread. The café was full of big Indians in tall twenty-gallon hats. Two girls came in and ordered coffee. They began to talk in

Navajo, a language that manages to sound both slurred and bitten off at the same time. Every once in a while, an English word would pop up in the soft stream of Athabascan: "basketball game," "Chevy pickup," "cheeseburger." One of the girls went over to the jukebox, put in a quarter and punched three songs: "Okie from Muskogee," "Purple Haze," and "Wasted Days and Wasted Nights" by Freddy Fender. Later that afternoon I picked up a hitchhiker, a kid on his way home to Kayenta: "My cousins and I started a rock-and-roll band," he told me. "We were doing great till Marvin got scared by witches and got sick."

Rob Schulteis has gone on to write good books on sports and the human body and on the war in Afghanistan. *The Hidden West* has its cult readers and rabid fans (among them more than a few of my students), but it doesn't have the readership it deserves. Only a few authors get as close as Schultheis does to the flesh and bones of the Southwest—Chuck Bowden, Tony Hillerman, Leslie Silko, maybe sometimes Ron Querry; on different subjects, Gary Nabhan and James Corbett. Ed Abbey and Aldo Leopold. He's *that* good.

Maybe on some cosmic scale it's just as well that thousands of fans of *The Hidden West* have not descended on its fragile landscapes. But then, those who love this book recognize one thing that it demonstrated: that everyone finds his or her own hidden West (South, North, East . . .). Meanwhile, it's my privilege to reintroduce this wonderful book.

—Stephen Bodio
Bozeman, MT

Crossing the Dry Line

I FIRST TRAVELED WEST IN THE SUMMER OF 1962. I WAS fresh out of prep school, and greenhorn and dumb as a kid can be. By "West" I mean the country beyond the 100th meridiàn, beyond Dodge City, Kansas, and Broken Bow, South Dakota, where the rainfall withers away to less than twenty inches a year: the American outback, which stretches all the way to the eastern edge of the Sierra Nevada in California. It is mystery country: terra incognita, a land of lost rivers, dead seas, track-less deserts, mountains charged with voodoo, adobe Lhasas at the end of endless roads. Even the names are like incantations: Paradox Valley; Shangri-la Canyon; Aladdin's Lamp Pass; the Last Chance Mountains. A hundred yards off the Interstate nothing has changed in 10,000 years: the land is Pleistocene, Neolithic, sunk in a Native American dream time.

I knew nothing of all that back then. I hitch-hiked from Amherst to New York, wearing a tweed jacket with a copy of On the Road in a pocket, lugging a big tan leather suitcase. In New York I spent forty of my last fifty dollars on a Greyhound ticket to Des Moines, Iowa. From Des Moines a day and a half later, I set out for Denver by thumb. I had no idea of what I was doing: my head was full of Kerouac, a West that never was, a country of scat-singing cowboys and jalopies full of poets screaming like shooting stars through the night. I hitched the curlicuing back roads, narrow ribbons of blacktop through farm towns like Elk Horn, Guthrie Center and Persia, rides of one or three or twenty miles that took me as far north or south as they did west. The countryside was gorgeous: corn fields rippled like sheets of iridescent green silk in the hot wind, and here and there grain elevators stuck up like rockets.

I spent the night with a tenant farmer and his wife in a big clapboard farmhouse with a potbellied wood-burning stove. The next day I hitched on, crossing the Missouri River just north of Omaha: raw bluffs, bleak timber, wild brown waters rolling south . . . It took the rest of the day to work my way another hundred miles into Nebraska. Subtly, the land was beginning to dry out. The greens in the landscape faded; the silos grew farther apart, then vanished; corn and pigs gave way to range, cattle. The air lost its sweet dung smell. The people took on a parched, windy look, mummies walking around in big cowboy hats.

That afternoon I rode south with a fat, merry diesel truck driver to Salina, Kansas; and from there (as the stars came out), two crazy young kids who had busted out of reform school—innocent prairie nihilists with pistols—drove me west through the night, stopping twice to siphon gas out of tractors parked in fields along the road.

At dawn the sun came up behind us, red and tremendous; and there were the Great Plains, rolling away endlessly in the four directions: grass, wheat stubble, parched rye, earth brown as a bruin. The horizons looked ankle-high, as if you might trip over them; there was nothing to grab on to. About noon the two gunsels dropped me off at Kit Carson—"We're headin' for LA!"—and I hitched from there up to Denver with an old rancher in a dusty, battered old black Ford pickup truck.

Sometime in the night, half dreaming, half awake, I had crossed the Dry Line, the 100th meridian. I didn't know it then, but at that moment my life had changed, forever; my past had slipped off me like a dead husk. Like John T. Unger in "The Diamond as Big as the Ritz," I had journeyed West through the depths of night and come to in a strange, strange land.

There is something in the country beyond the Dry Line, in the vastness and emptiness of it, that resists knowing. The old cartographers and explorers—Cabeza de Vaca, Jedediah Smith, Fremont, Pike, Lewis and Clark—all were *lost*, sleepwalking across a continent of their own imagining. Were they knocking on the back door to China? Were there seven xanthic cities beyond those distant horizons of dread rock? What lay beyond those snowy mountain ranges? Or were they only summer clouds?

I knew no more than they did. Totally lost myself, I rode toward Denver across the rolling plains, into the great mystery.

The
Great Plains

FOR A WHILE I LIVED IN A CABIN NORTH OF BOULDER, ON THE very edge of the Great Plains, with the foothills of the Rockies at its back. The Plains Cabin, it was called; it had been built back in the twenties by a mad old man, one more rancher with his wits blown out of his skull by the wind. It was a weird house, built out of scrap lumber and ill-fitted remnants of other, long-gone houses, shacks, sheds and barns: a drab patchwork house, with the same weather-bleached color you see in old houses by the sea. Living in the Plains Cabin, in fact, was a lot like living on a desolate coast, some such place as Newfound land, Iceland, the Hebrides. From my front door the plains stretched away like the sea; at night the tiny lights of cars bobbed like dories out in the swells of the rolling hills; every morning I found coyote tracks around the sides of the house, like the arcane signs and things you find at dawn on a beach, left by the tide.

The Plains Cabin was as close as I would ever want to get to actually living on the plains: it is just too lonely a place. If the Great Plains had an anthem, it would be played on a broken tom-tom by an Indian dying of smallpox, accompanied by an Okie on a harmonica full of dust. Its banner would be an American flag with buffalo skulls for stars. When I think of the plains, I think of exile, abandonment, extinction.

I recall one winter dusk up in the Dakotas, in a small cow town. My car had broken down, and I had sold it, and now I was waiting for a bus to take me to Cheyenne and on down to Denver. The bus station, which was also the hotel lobby and the only café and saloon in town, was full of cowboys and Indians on their way to places like Recluse, Lodge Grass and Verdigris. I started talking to a solemn cowpoke carrying a battered suitcase and a carefully coiled lariat. "I'm from Okla-homa," he told me. "I saved up my rodeo winnings and bought a fine little ranch, beef cattle and horses, close by the Texas border. My wife found out she couldn't have children and it broke her heart. She left home, ran away—left me a note that said good-bye. I've been looking for her ever since. I've been everywhere: New York, Chicago, New Orleans, Los Angeles, Denver—I've hitch-hiked all over the country, showin' folks her picture, asking them if they seen her. Sometimes somebody has—she works as a short-order waitress—but she's always moved on. I'll look for her till I find her."

He was a lean and fine-looking man; I expected his wife must have been lovely, some mythical beauty, to inspire his two years' search. But then he took his wallet out and carefully pulled out her photograph, a ragged color snapshot: there she was, colossal, more lumps than a sack of potatoes, smiling in pin curls, a tentlike blouse, bulging slacks. An Indian named Deo Grass had been listening to the cowboy's story; he looked at the picture, took the Bull Durham cigarette out of his mouth and chuckled. "Shouldn't be hard to find *her!*"

Exile, abandonment, extinction: the buffalo, of course, are the paradigmatic case. In the mid-nineteenth century there were still 50 million of them roaming the prairies; thirty years later there were fewer than 1,000. They were killed for their sweet tongue meat, for their hides, to starve out the Indians who depended on them, and, simply, because they were wild. The final stage of the extermination process was the bone trade: wandering whites and Indians burned off the prairie grass to expose the buffalo skeletons, gathered them by the wagonload and stacked them along the railroad lines for shipment east, where they were used as fertilizer and in the refining of sugar. There are accounts of bone ricks twelve feet high and a quarter of a mile long. Two and a half million dollars in buffalo bones. No wonder the plains are haunted.

Once, in memory of what was gone, I bought three pounds of buffalo meat in a store. I cut it in thin strips; held up to the light, they looked like ribbons of rough amber glass. I turned the oven on to 150 degrees, laid the strips of meat on racks, put them in the oven and left the door open a crack. Hours later I brought them out, brittle and light as balsam wood. I spent the rest of the day crumbling them up and pounding them into dust with a mortar and pestle. It was hard to believe, when I was finished, that the powder had ever been flesh; it looked mineral—a rare earth, dry, vitreous and silver. I took it with me on several long, hard journeys. A pinch of the stuff exploded in my throat into a wild red thunderbolt of meat: a Native American communion.

One day, years ago, an anthropologist friend gave me a name and address on a piece of paper. John Strange Bear, my friend said, was perhaps the last great medicine man in the Dakotas. A few years back, there had been several great medicine men, but one had died in a car wreck on the way home from a sun dance; another was blind and voiceless in an old folks' home in Rapid City; and another was touring the college lecture circuit and wanted Marlon Brando to star in a movie version of his life. Strange Bear, my friend said, was the real thing; an inheritor of the traditions of Crazy Horse and Black Elk, all of those wise men, those celestial comedians and chemists of vision whose lineage went far, far back into the Stone Age. This magic had come across the Bering Sea from Asia, with the paleo-Indian hunters, 30,000 years ago. If anyone knew the old secrets, it was this man, Strange Bear.

I had always been curious about the Indians of the Great Plains. I had gotten to know a crowd of Oklahoma Indians, Kiowas, Pawnees and southern Cheyennes who had moved to Denver and Boulder to work and go to school. They were full of tales of pow-wows, gourd and sun dances, and Saturday-night Indian wars, jalopies prowling the back roads, headlights off, bristling with deer rifles.

One guy, Tommy Nighthawk, went home to Anadarko for a visit and came back to Denver with black, swollen eyes. He had had a few drinks and went to a big intertribal fair where he ran into four Pawnees. Tommy was a Cheyenne; he hated Pawnees, who had fought on the side of the white man in the

Indian wars; he decided to kill the four Pawnees with his bare hands. He was doing a pretty good job of it when four Oklahoma highway patrolmen showed up; and he was whomping them too (so he said) when they knocked him down and maced him seven times right in the eyes. They hauled him off to jail. He came to in the cell, went mad and began to sing his death song. He beat his head against the bars until he cracked his skull. They tear-gassed him, put him in a strait jacket and shot him full of Thorazine. The next morning they hauled him in front of the judge. The judge told him he was charged with drunkenness, attempted murder, assault on police officers and attempted suicide. Told him to get out of Anadarko and not come back. "We'll shoot you on sight," they said. They took Tommy to the airport in manacles and marched him up to the Denver plane. He turned around at the top of the ramp. "I'm comin' back," he said.

Tommy and his friends were warriors without a war; and they still held to the animistic beliefs of their grandfathers. The plains, they said, were an American Holy Land. Down in their part of Oklahoma there were still shrines and places of power: wan, burned hills full of rattlesnakes and revelations; creeks in the Canadian River country where you could scoop an antediluvian snapping turtle out of the mud and read the future in the endless jade whorls of his shell; knolls and nodular buttes where you just didn't go, for Something dwelled there—not evil, not good, just *Something* that sucked away men's reason. They told of old people who could call bears: call a keening, atonal song out into the night, and after a while a bear would come, loping and snuffling, with a message. These tales fascinated me. Visiting Mr. Strange Bear, I thought, might give me at least a glimpse of a corner of this old world.

The spring I set out for the Dakotas was a wet, stormy one. The snow had barely melted on the plains and already there were thunderstorms. Tornadoes were reported here and there. Driving north, I saw that the low-lying fields along the highway were flooded; ragged lines of geese sculled across the sky. A fox red as rust darted away through the green, green grass. I imagined horsemen against the horizon, painted, feathered, yelling their dissonant songs. It must have been glorious to be an Indian, I thought, during that frail golden age of horses and guns. Ah, but such things never last for long.

I drove across the gnomic badlands of southeastern Wyoming, across the upper reaches of the North Platte, and then I turned east into Nebraska, through the Sand Hills. The Sand Hills are . . . well, *improbable*—they shouldn't really exist. More on them later.

I turned north across the state line into South Dakota, and then I was in Indian country—the Pine Ridge Sioux Reservation. The road coiled through more hills, past rough-hewn farmhouses, cabins, an occasional rickety trailer; here and there, cottonwoods chimed with birds, like elaborate calliopes. Angular cattle grazed on a rocky hillside; I passed a rude log corral with three shaggy bison peering out. When the road climbed out onto the hilltops, the country was suddenly boundless, spinning slowly around me, clouds piled at the far edges. A school bus went by, going the other way, its windows full of delicate brown children who stared at me with soft, shining eyes. It was not a long way to Wounded Knee from there: Wounded Knee, where the U.S. Army slaughtered three hundred unarmed Dakotas, mostly women and children, on December 29, 1890. It was hard not to feel uneasy, a stranger.

I gassed up at a lonely reservation crossroads store, and continued north, then west again, through Wanblee, and on. The road turned to dirt, mud, crossing prairie as green as a mantis. I drove through a place I'll call Prairie Dog Town, and another place I'll call Six Logs. The road worsened. It was afternoon now, and thunder rumbled in the distance. I was traversing the very edge of the Badlands. To the north, the prairie crumbled off into pale sandstone buttes and rococo cliffs; disquieting country, the kind you visit in dreams.

The road took a last crook, and there it was, as my friend had described it: a flat stretch of prairie between two hills, with a cluster of cabins and trailers, a round corral and a litter of broken-down cars and trucks, black and bleeding rust on the green Indian grass. Strange Bear's camp.

Edmund Carpenter, the anthropologist and filmmaker,

quotes an Eskimo woman as saying, "We believe that people can live a life apart from real life." The man I saw standing in front of the cabin reminded me of that. He was pale, for a Lakota, and slim and sleek as an ermine. He stood out, somehow, like an enamel figurine. His face was sharp and fine, almost girlish; his hair, black, silky, must have hung two feet long down his back. He wore muddy Can't-Bust-'Em overalls, high-top logger's gum boots and a Caterpillar cap; when he shook my hand, his grip was hard and calloused. His gaze was disquietingly steady, like a movie gunfighter's. There was something strange about his voice, too, when he said hello and asked me who I was and how the drive up from Colorado had been. I couldn't put my finger on it at first, and then I realized that his inflections were all off: he talked like Bela Lugosi as Dracula, as if he were reciting a language he did not understand. A horse whinnied in the corral and ran in a tight, skidding circle, spooked, I guess, by the smell of a *wasichu,* a white man.

The thunderheads to the north were darkening, bruised with rain. We went inside the nearest cabin and sat down at the kitchen table. The floor was hard-beaten earth; the walls looked as if they had been assembled from four different sources and nailed uneasily together. The kitchen shelves were covered with poverty food, USDA cans and sacks of potatoes. Strange Bear put on a big pot of coffee. "My wife left me," he said. "She ran off to Rapid City to drink. She said there's no money in the medicine man business and nothing to do out here." He laughed. "Money drives people crazy."

Medicine men do not seem to fit our common notions of human behavior, our logic; they slip like elvers through our weirs of analysis. Crazy Horse, for instance. (His real name was "He dreamt he was riding through a battle on a strange horse, riding slowly through the bullets and arrows; because of the horse's magic, he could not be harmed.") Crazy Horse's ability to predict the future was so reliable that his people used it to plan military strategy against the *wasichus*. Crazy Horse once predicted that the only thing that could kill him was steel in the hands of a fellow Dakota. He was slain by an Indian policeman wielding a bayonet, fulfilling the prophecy. There are no photographs or portraits of Crazy Horse, and no one knows where he is buried: like King Arthur, or Merlin, or the Mahdi of Shiite Islam, he is not dead, not really. He is the eternal returner, the Once and Future Medicine Man.

Strange Bear talked and talked as we sat at that skewed table on tipsy stools, drinking coffee syrupy with sugar and eating stew of salt beef and potatoes. Was he being funny, or was he serious? I couldn't tell. I had wanted to ask him all about the holy places in the Badlands, over in the Black Hills and the surrounding prairies—naïve, presumptuous questions—but I never got the chance. The FBI was after him, he said, because of his involvement in the Wounded Knee occupation. Was I an FBI man? If so, he would read my mind and find out. But it didn't matter. *Nothing* could stop him, because he was a full-blooded Dakota—not like that Mr. Two Crows down the road. Two Crows *said* he was pureblood, but his eyes weren't Indian eyes and he was half bald. Whoever heard of a bald-headed Indian? You couldn't trust halfbreeds; besides, they were all racists. They were more white inside than Indian, and everyone knew how crazy and racist whites were. Someday a virus would come and wipe out all the white people and spare all the Indians and everything would be okay again . . . "Here, have some more stew," Strange Bear said. "There's plenty."

The grass outside was full of crickets singing like a thousand tiny bicycle bells. When we left the house, the last dusk light was gone, and there was nothing but darkness and masses of fiery stars above. The landscape was black, with not a light beyond Strange Bear's little camp. An owl called somewhere down in the cottonwoods along the crick, and the Indian cocked his head to the sound. I thought I saw him smile. "This place is full of the spirits of my people," he said. "They are in the trees and grasses." His voice was soft and he sounded like a completely different person. "You can hear them in the night, if you are real quiet." He paused, and again the owl hooted from the wooded draw.

The next morning I rose early and walked down behind the camp and across the little creek. From there the grasslands rolled north—forever, it seemed. I skirted the sun-dance circle, a rough fence of dried brown pine boughs where Strange Bear gave a sun dance every summer. Don't go in the sun-dance circle, he had warned me the night before, so I did not.

The sky was tremendous now, boiling with silver clouds. The prairie was a carpet of grasses and weeds, thistles and flowers and thorns. (This prairie, I had read somewhere, had originally, aboriginally, been an intricate fretwork of woven plants: peppergrass, saltgrass, grama grass, porcupine grass, buffalo grass, prairie June grass, cat's foot, hairy golden aster, skeleton weed, lamb's-tongue, wolfberry, knotweed, mustard, chokecherry, strawberry, pennyroyal. Now it survived only in a few isolated places like this. Most of the Great Plains had been ploughed under and replanted with foreign hybrid grasses and grains.)

Two great moths, their wings fantastic, like mosaics of radioactive ore, fucked on a dry stalk of weed. I rounded another forbidden place Strange Bear had described to me, a bluff where, he had said, so many medicine men had gotten visions that the place was dangerously loaded with spiritual power. "A young kid wandered up here one time by mistake," he said, "and the thunder got a hold of him, and when he came down he was forty miles west of here and he smelled like electricity."

I walked and walked, feeling a giddy kind of ecstasy; and the farther I walked the more I understood, or thought I understood, Strange Bear. There was a raw, inchoate power in this country, and it poured through the man like an explosion of light through a prism, casting mad colors. It was too much to expect sense out of it.

Passing a lone cottonwood, I came to a steep escarpment running north to south, where the grass fell away, and peered down into a jigsaw puzzle of gullies and hummocks that looked as if it had been sculpted out of clay and lime and rock salt: the Badlands. A deer trail, fresh tracks, led down to a ravine and disappeared. There was an indefinable feeling of *something* out there in those strange calcareous hills. I felt a prickling at the back of my neck; something almost but not quite visible stirred the corner of my eye. I turned my gaze west: a red-tailed hawk was slipping low down over the curve of the land, hunting.

When I got back to camp it was almost dusk. Strange Bear was arguing with another Sioux man, half in English, half in Dakota. The other man, short and stumpy, in sunglasses and mechanic's overalls, wanted to pull a fuel pump off one of the wrecked trucks and put it on his own pickup. John refused to give it to him: "You still owe me for that carburetor!" Mister Stumpy accused John of acting like a sour-faced Anglo. John told Stumpy that if he didn't drink so much wine over in Pierre, maybe he could afford to *buy* himself a new fuel pump.

I wandered off a ways in the gathering dark, and sat in the tall grass till I heard Stumpy's pickup start up, and saw the headlights crawl out to the road and turn north toward the highway, and Pierre. When I got back to the cabin, Strange Bear was already eating dinner, the same coffee and stew as the night before. "My father was a medicine man before me," he said. "That man there, he could have been one too. But too much boozing, too much wine—drinking up in Pierre. You can be a falling-down drunk and still be a medicine man, but you have to be free of the stuff. You can't let it drive you.

"I did the Sun Dance four times." He pulled back his ragged workshirt to show the big, puckered scars, bone white against the dark hematitic skin, where the skewers had torn loose; it made me grit my teeth. "I did four visionfasts. They say when you do your fifth visionfast, you just disappear. Maybe I'll do that someday soon." He chuckled.

"I can't tell you about this country around here. Not because you're a white man; you're just in too big a hurry. It takes a whole year to get ready for a visionfast. You have to get a woman to sew you a star blanket to wear. You have to gather different kinds of herbs from all over; some of them are very hard to find. You have to learn to speak Lakota—the spirits around here all speak Lakota, and what if they came to you in the night and you couldn't understand a word they were saying? Then, all kinds of dangerous things happen on a visionfast. You might go crazy, or you might drop dead, or the Thunder People might decide to take you away with them, and nobody would ever see you again.

"Even if you get a vision, so what? A vision and a quarter will buy you a cup of coffee. Nobody cares about visions any more. Too bad."

Perhaps I should have stayed on there a while, through the brilliant summer at least, learning, accreting the slow, hard nodular layers of magic. But it was just too hard. I thought about it that night: imagined myself becoming somebody different, a Dakota tongue in my mouth, a wizard's flinty heart in my breast . . . No. The next morning, early, I headed south, home, for Denver.

It was beyond me; it is hard enough just *living* out on the plains, on those blank, analphabetic hills. The plains can break your spirit. The wind howls through you as if you were a skeleton, nails you to a Cross of Ice, and it never stops: one of the windiest spots on earth is on the western edge of the plains, a place called Rocky Flats, Colorado. I lived near there for ten years, and I never got used to the wind. It blew so hard it made your teeth ache; it bullied the landscape, hurling dust and pushing hills, houses and trees around.

If the wind doesn't get you, the distances will. Radar operators who stare too long at their sets are prone to a disease of the mind called *radar fever*: they begin to see things, fantastical things—fiery angels, Cheshire cat smiles, Ezekiel's wheel, squadrons of skulls with diamond eyes. The same thing happens to the plains dweller. Perhaps that accounts for the plains Indians' voracious hunger for visions, their manic questing: lost, dried out, hollowed by the wind, you yearn and wander and search, like that poor cowboy looking for his low-rent Eurydice.

If the mysteries of the Great Plains have a heartland, it is the Sand Hills of Nebraska. The Sand Hills stretch two hundred miles east to west, from the valley of the North Platte in the south to the Black Hills and Badlands of South Dakota in the north. They are one of the great deserts of the world, an American Rub al Khali or Gobi. A desert in disguise: walk out of Valentine, Cody, Whiteclay, Chadron—one of those ephemeral little Sand Hills cow towns whose main street looks like a painted stage set with nothing behind it—and dig. Beneath the brittle grass and the thin smoke of soil, you hit sand; you are standing in a sea of dunes. And if you dig deep enough, you will come to an even stranger realm: a vast ancient subterranean ocean, the 156,000-square-mile Ogallala Aquifer, with more water in it than Lake Huron. A sea inside a desert wrapped in a green prairie.

Anyone who has driven across the country on Interstate 80 has seen the Sand Hills: if you look north from Ogallala or North Platte, they are the dim, miragelike hummocks along the horizon. But almost no one knows anything about them. Crazy Horse died in the Sand Hills, at a place called Fort Robinson, near present-day Chadron. A century ago the Sand Hills were the Serengeti of America: the prairies and marshes teemed with buffalo, prairie wolves, whole prides of mountain lions; in the eighteenth and nineteenth centuries, the fur trappers worked the headwaters of rivers such as the Leup, the Elkhorn and the Niobrara, and lakes like Moon, Hackberry and Pelican. Most of the big game is gone now, but deer and coyote are still found in the draws, down in the pocket forests of willow, cottonwood, ash and plum; turkey vultures, golden eagles and red tails still ride the skies.

I had a friend who was born in the Sand Hills country and grew up there on a cattle ranch north of Ogallala. Her name was Martha Schaller, and her family, German-American, had moved to western Nebraska from Minnesota two generations ago, back in the 1880s. They had started out as sodbusters: Martha's great-grandfather dug a pit house out of the prairie soil and roofed it with a canvas tent the first winter they were there. He wanted to farm, but the best farmland, down in the North Platte Valley, was already taken, so he took to cattle ranching. The family owned 12,000 acres, two thirds of it range, the other third creek bottom irrigated with walls. Martha was six feet tall and weighed about a hundred pounds, still wore the Levi jacket she had gotten for her thirteenth birthday, smoked little black cigars and had been a model in Paris. Her childhood was a honky-tonk fairy tale. Her grandfather flew his own plane until he was eighty years old, cruising down to Mexico with his cronies to hunt, fish and carouse. Her mother had gotten mad at her father ten years ago and hadn't said a word since: she communicated by writing notes. The hills around the ranch, where Martha rode her pony when she was a little girl, were full of enigmas. Once as she rode home at winter dusk in a swirling Great Plains blizzard, her horse spooked and she looked up and saw (she said) an enormous white wolf, three feet high at the shoulder, leap the barbed-wire fence and race away across the white prairie. There was also an eroded sandstone bluff back in the hills, and when you crawled in with a flashlight you found yourself in a vault that went as high as fifty feet in places. And there were bats: tens of thousands of the ruby-eyed little leather devils hanging upside down. It was like crawling into hell.

One summer when Martha went home to visit, she told her father she was going to ride out to the bat cave the next day, for old time's sake. "You won't find nothin'," he said. "Why not?" she asked. "Well, a couple of years back, we had a rabies scare in the county—skunks, wild dogs, coons. I wasn't sure but what the bats might have it too, so Ed Weicker and I went up there and dynamited the entrance." He laughed. "There's nothin' there but a big old pile of rocks."

It was as if that was the beginning of the end, Martha said. The wells started to run dry a couple of years later, wells that had been giving sweet cold water since 1890. They drilled new ones, but half of them came up dry; they hired a water dowser, but he got bit by a rattlesnake and went back to Cheyenne. It was the same all across the Great Plains, from Rocky Boys Cree Reservation to Levelland, Texas: the Ogallala Aquifer, the mysterious hidden sea that made farming and ranching on the plains possible, was drying up. Geologists and hydrologists said it was because of the cities—Denver, Wichita, Lubbock and the rest. They were pumping water out of the aquifer faster than the rain and snowmelt could replace it, pumping it out and using it on lawns and golf courses and suburban parks.

The last time Martha went home to visit, she found her father sitting at his desk with a half-empty bottle of Jack Daniel's and a mess of farm journals and scientific reports. It's all over, he told her. Sand Hills cattle ranching's dead. We've got maybe thirty years left, and then the whole business is going to dry up and blow away; from Denver to the hundredth meridian, this country's gonna look like Afghanistan. The dirt farmer and the rancher's gonna be as gone as fifty million buffalo, as dead as Crazy Horse, as rare as a set of jackalope antlers. Ed Weicker and I and every other rancher in this county should have crawled in that cave with the goddamn bats and dynamited the door down from the inside.

Exile, abandonment, extinction. Plains history is like an opera: everyone gets killed in the end, singing as they die. The Mandan, for instance: they lived in fortified villages of earth lodges on the upper Missouri River, raising corn and hunting buffalo from horseback. Catlin painted them; one masterpiece shows their gorgeous bear dance, with men in masks leaping and stamping. From all accounts the Mandan were stolid, blunt, canny people, rather like the Pueblo Indians of the Southwest; villagers, Neolithic burghers. A French Canadian trader who hated Indians (inexplicably, he was married to a Mandan woman) sold them smallpox-infected blankets; within a generation, the tribe died off. There are terrible tales from travelers of this time, of villages full of the dead and dying, drums thudding in the night, trying to drive the disease away; of shamans dreaming new songs and rites to try to cure the sick, murdered by their tribesmen when the cures failed; of village after village silent, bones scattered in the fields. Only a score or so of Mandan descendants survive among the Arickaree of North Dakota today, and their culture and language are lost forever.

Then, the Kickapoos. They began on the prairies of Illinois; they were driven from there to Kansas, and from Kansas to Texas, and finally to Mexico. A band of them still lives in the Great Mexican Desert, outside of a town called Nueva Rosita, ruled over by a shaman-chief named Papiquano. Another band lives near Shawnee, Oklahoma. Every year the entire Mexican Kickapoo Nation, four hundred-odd souls, crosses the border into the United States, where they work as migrant farm laborers during the summer. The Kickapoos have no passports; they are neither Americans nor Mexicans. Many of them cross the border between Piedras Negras and Eagle Pass, Texas, carrying photostats of an 1832 letter written by a Major Whittle, U.S. Army, giving them safe conduct in the United States. They will have nothing to do with us.

There is a constant sense of loss on the plains. Reason, iron, will not avail there. The ghost dance, the true religion of America, finds its truest expression on the plains. Founded by Wovokah (AKA Jack Wilson), a Nevada Piute, in the 1870s, the ghost dance preached that if you prayed, danced, sang, hard enough, the dead would rise. Dead Indians, extinct animals—they would all rise, and the old, wild America would live again; dusty brown rivers of buffalo, wolf, lynx, peregrine, antelope, raven, sawwhet owl, its eyes like gold foil. Peel back the black earth, and there would be the ghostly fetuses, glimmering like mother-of-pearl, waiting to be born. The ghost dance died in the winter of 1890 at Wounded Knee; but there are rumors that it persists back in the Badlands, in the cracked, sallow hills . . .

Why not? It makes as much sense as anything out on the plains.

Someday I will have to go back there, to the Sand Hills, or the Llano Estacado, or one of the other lost archipelagos out on that withered sea of earth. Perhaps to the Little Missouri

Grasslands; I have an obscure U.S. government map of the place that looks like it was drawn by Borges or Lewis Carroll. Places such as Hidatsa Village; Lone Grave; Mary (1908); Poker Jim Cemetery; Adobe Wall; Bicycle; Sophie's Nipples; The Last Buffalo Hunt in North Dakota. Looking at the map, I imagine a tall nineteenth-century bicycle on a grassy hilltop in the wind; a few miles away, Sophie lies naked on a brass bed on another lonely hilltop; while nearby, Indians in plumed top hats, riding horses and Model T Fords, wave rifles and whiskey bottles as they chase buffaloes from horizon to horizon, a chase that never ends . . .

In a way, it would be a shame to spoil such a wonderful map by actually going there and seeing the places themselves; but then again, on the plains my dreams may even fall short of the strangeness I find waiting out there.

The Last Canyon: Notes from the Underground

WHEN I FINALLY MOVED FROM THE EDGE OF THE GREAT Plains across the continental divide to the western slope of the Rockies, it was purely by chance. The construction crew I was working on in Denver was laid off for the winter, and I gave up, for the fourth and last time, on my anthropology Ph.D. thesis. A friend called me from San Miguel County, down in the south-western corner of Colorado: she had found an old sheep-herder's cabin, rent-free, and did I want to come down and help her fix it up? I threw everything I owned, which wasn't much, in the back of my van, stuffed my last four hundred dollars in my jeans and headed west across the Great Divide. It never occurred to me that I might be on some kind of pilgrimage or quest, but I was: further into the nether lands of the West. The best pilgrimages are like that, lucky accidents.

The sheepherder's cabin, scrap wood and tarpaper with a tin roof, stood in a grove of aspens 9,000 feet up on a mesa top above an old mining town called Telluride. The mountain wind beat against the door and piled snow in knee-deep drifts against the west wall. There was a shallow sickle of a tarn below the aspens; the water from the tarn ran off through a culvert under the highway and then tumbled down through the woods into the south fork of the San Miguel River. This was alpine country, ponderosa pine and Doug fir and aspen, rising to snow-streaked granite peaks, jagged teeth of gray and rose. It was gold and silver country, and the mountainsides bled heaps of blighted rubble where the mines and glory holes had been. In the winter the county was opulent with snow: moun-tains of diamond and opal, snow to the gunwales of the car as you ricocheted down icy roads through white timber.

There is a wonderful children's book by Holling Clancy Holling titled *Paddle-to-the-Sea*. It tells how a Canadian Indian boy carves a wooden figurine of a man in a canoe and leaves it on the side of a snowy hill near Lake Superior. When the snow melts in the springtime, the little boat is carried on a long, long journey through beaver swamps, streams, the Great Lakes and out into the Atlantic Ocean, where it drifts all the way to the Grand Banks: a romance of random drifting, of magical flotsam and jetsam.

Splitting the big logs for the stove in the little shack by the lake—the hearts of the logs were white as marble, with a turpentiney stench—I imagined a sliver of that high mountain wood traveling down with the snow water: crossing the tarn in a spring squall, riding the San Miguel down out of the Rockies through the deep gorges and mesa country, being dragged down through the depths of the continent by the mighty Colorado River itself and, finally, washing out through the delta into the Sea of Cortez. It was a journey that was no longer possible: there were too many dams in the way, backing the river up into a series of stagnant lakes. But in the mind, at least, one could still carve one's runes in the native wood and send it down to the sea and beyond.

My cabin sat on the eastern edge of the Colorado Plateau. To the west lay the long, tilted mesas, separated by deep gorges, which make up the western edge of the Rockies; and beyond, the canyon country of Utah, intricately carved with so many canyons, buttes, arroyos, cones, spires, monoliths and domes that you could, as they say, pull it out flat and it wouldn't fit on the map.

If the overwhelming feature of the Great Plains is grass, on the Colorado Plateau it is *rock,* naked, unadorned geology—old sea floors, petrified sand dunes, the dried blood of long-gone volcanoes. This was the country I found myself drawn to. I lived in the mountains, but the desert, the canyon country, drew me irresistibly.

My favorite place for a long time was a certain part of the San Juan River country. The San Juan begins on Wolf Creek Pass, in southwestern Colorado; becomes Navaho Lake, a desperately ugly reservoir, in northern New Mexico; flows on, picking up the tributary waters of Mancos Creek, the Rio Animas (River of Souls), the Chaco; crosses the burnt sageland around Shiprock, Aneth and Bluff, on the borderline between the Navaho Nation and the Mormon country; and then descends into a deep, winding gorge, with side canyons and arroyos feathering down out of the mesa country around Monument Valley and Navaho Mountain.

This is the wildest part of the San Juan River system, and one of the wildest places in the world. There are canyons down there that are like passages back in time. One is reminded of the words of the physicist Hermann Minkowski, who said, "Henceforth space by itself, and time by itself, are doomed to fade away into mere shadows, and only a kind of union of the two will preserve an independent reality." Hiking down an arroyo, following it down as it becomes a chasm, one recapitulates the whole of America's past. You break through the Iron Age, thin and brilliant as an oil slick, and descend through the Navaho, the Piute, the Anasazi and the Basketmaker down into, finally, the prehuman bedrock of the continent.

For years I had known of a certain side canyon of the San Juan that was supposed to be particularly lovely, a place resonant with power and almost untrodden. The woman who told me about it was a beautiful desert rat, sunburnt dark, with quick, clear eyes; she knew the canyon country like the lines in her hard hands. She drew me a map on a paper napkin in a café in El Paso and made me promise not to tell anyone else about it. In return I gave her directions to a river of hot sulfur water in the eastern California desert, far up a ravine in the hills. A trade, place for place.

Somehow I didn't go there for a long, long time; it was one of those trips you save up—like a lump of pemmican or a last gold coin—against hard times. I kept the map, folded into a tiny square, with a bundle of old photographs, letters, chips of nacre from Mexican beaches, a zigzagged shard from Keet Seel, the long-deserted pueblo city north of Black Mesa, beyond Skeleton Canyon. That scrawled scrap of a map was something like a talisman, evoking the luminous energy of the woman who had drawn it (I never saw her again) and the mystery, the promise, of her canyon.

And then one autumn, suddenly it was time to go. October in Colorado, and the sun had been snuffed out by sleet and rain. It had been trying to snow for four days straight. Something seemed to be wrong: the stars crossed, the yarrow stalks mis-cued. The world was closing in: bad debts, a tangled love, a pulled knee that ate two muzzy grains of codeine a day and still hurt. It was a mournful season. The aspens glowed like hills of candles in the clouds; the scrub brush along the river was Siberian amber. The papers were full of the usual bad news, so bad, so usual, that it almost made you laugh. The oil crisis was getting worse again, and no one knew what to do about it, if anything. The dollar was falling like a shooting star, and some people were predicting a nightmare like Germany in the twen-ties, hundred-dollar bills worthless as dead leaves drifting away in the wind. It seemed a good time to leave, to evacuate this luciferin century and descend into deeper, stiller times.

Fall is a good season to go into the San Juan desert. In the summer, temperatures rise above 110 degrees, the sun batters all color and shadow out of the land, and springs, seeps and waterholes dry up. Water is the great mystery out here: you see why the Indians made rain a sacrament, the wet mountains the abode of gods, and springs into shrines. *All* water—brackish, saline, stale—is holy water.

The whole land is *shaped* like water—combers of slick rock, tumbled surfs of tumulus, whirlpools of dust and sand—but the stuff itself is elusive, lost. There is rainfall and runoff and the spring snowmelt, but these are rare, scant things. Somewhere far, far below in the knotted depths of stone, the San Juan rolls down its subterranean gorge, deep with the rains and snows of the Rockies; but up in the side canyons it is bone dry. The air is burnt, sharp as a steel knife laid on the tongue. You feel as though you could sniff out a glass of water blindfolded at a hundred yards. Walking, your fingers swell and turn a bruised yellow in a couple of hours. Your mind wanders to chimeras, gauzy things of the imagination. No wonder so many religions began in the desert! Even with a couple of full canteens gurgling in your pack, the thought of thirst is never really absent. And yet, you can just as easily drown or freeze to death in these same canyons. Sometimes it seems that the San Juan is imbued with a sly, native sense of humor, the soul of a coyote. It turns you into jerky one day and freeze-dries you the next; dries you out, then drowns you. I once got caught by a March blizzard down there, with a wind chill factor somewhere way below zero, snowflakes thick and wet, whipping like tiny daggers up canyon. I hiked on, went into extreme hypothermia and survived only by hunching in a cave out of the wind, building a fire out of damp sticks and driftwood and standing over it while the steam poured off my soaked clothing. The next day the snow melted and the canyon ran waist-deep with icy water; you could have drowned in some of the big pools. Two days later the sky was hot and clear, the snowmelt had vanished and I trudged through dry sand looking for drinking water in the shadow of boulders in the lee of the cliffs. It is a maddening and wondrous place, the San Juan.

But now it was autumn—a sweet, easy season in the desert—and it was time to go, to follow that old fragment of map, to see where it led.

I had a friend at the time, a tiny woman named Susan, who lived alone in a cabin in the hills and worked silver for a living. She was a tough little person: she had banged the cabin together herself out of scrap lumber, and every year she shot an elk, out of season, and lived on the meat through the winter. She also had an ancient Chevy pickup truck that seemed as if it might make it to Utah and back. One part of me wanted to go walk the canyon alone: a kind of walking vision-seeking, like the traditional Plains Indians used to do. (It is interesting that in both Japanese Zen and Plains Indian animism, there are walking and sitting forms of contemplation.) Alone, I would be meeting the canyon solely on its own terms. But I was more than a little in love with Susan; and she would be a good person to walk the canyon with: she was spare with her words, and a hard walker. Like all real hunters, she fit into the country with no false notes, unobtrusive. She would be a good companion, I thought.

One colorless, drizzling dawn, we loaded up her truck with gear: packs, bags, canteens and concentrated foods—bulghur, lemonade mix, brown rice, Japanese noodles, dried fruit, tinned meat, tea—even a couple of bottles of wine. It was early, the town was still lit, there were spangles of ice in the road. We drove west, feeling like escaping prisoners.

The rain ended around Sawpit, and up on the mesas around Norwood where the big ranches begin, it was merely cloudy and cold. The autumn colors were delicate, like those of a Sung scroll. The Japanese have a word, "aware," which means a kind of beauty made more intense, poignant, by its very impermanence: beauty catalyzed by time into something almost unbearable. It was one of those autumn days in the mountains.

We drove west into Utah, skirting the southern edge of the La Sal Mountains, aspens gold, a thin frost of snow on the tops of the peaks. At La Sal Junction we turned south into the sandstone country. This is one of the last strongholds of old-fashioned Mormon ranching, where the church rules with an almost feudal power. The men are mostly gaunt, with short-cropped hair and miraculously sculpted sideburns; the women favor tall, blue or blond beehives. Time seems to have stopped somewhere in the late forties or early fifties down here, with a shot of the 1860s thrown in for good measure. But the people are friendly enough, in a taciturn way: they crack their smiles stingily and seldom laugh, as if outright joy would somehow expend their *mana*, their power.

In the last few years the Navahos, with their exploding population, have been moving north into Mormon land. The Mormons aren't all that comfortable about it. In Mormon mythology Indians are supposed to be one of the Twelve Lost Tribes of Israel, which means they are Chosen People, but you wouldn't necessarily want your daughter to marry one. The Navahos, on the other hand, like all expanding nations (their tribe has grown from fewer than 10,000 to nearly 200,000 in less than a century), are filled with a feisty confidence. When the pseudo-Indian film *Billy Jack* was shown in one of the little Mormon-Navaho towns in southeastern Utah a couple of years ago, Navaho teen-agers, inspired by the film's simple politics, stoned police cars and burned a gas station. It is an interesting eddy in the flood of history: a Native American manifest destiny.

Susan and I drove south, past the hogans of the northernmost Navahos and through the Ute town of White Rock; and then, somewhere south of the Abajo, or Blue, Mountains, we turned west again. To the east Sleeping Ute Mountain peered over the horizon, opal blue. Far, far to the southwest, Navaho Mountain was jade, in a black plume of rain. To the south the Lukachukai and Chuskai mountains and the rusty turrets and minarets of Monument Valley were dim in the haze; to the west, ferrous cliffs. The sky had broken and it was a cool, lucid afternoon; cumulus clouds sailed like a fleet of giant luminous cauliflowers across the sky.

We turned off the highway onto a dirt road that cut away across the flats, through sagebrush and scrub juniper. If it hadn't been for the map, we never would have seen it. The road forked and forked again, and got worse; we bumped down into a dry wash and out again. Feral cattle spooked and trotted away through the chaparral in whirlwinds of dust.

The road petered out, became a track. Before us, all was stony flatlands, brush; our canyon had hidden itself well.

We parked the truck in the shade of a lone cottonwood, shouldered our packs and started walking, wandering across the featureless terrain. Anyone following us would have thought we were lost; but after about half an hour, trusting to the vague markings on the map, we came to the beginnings of an arroyo cutting south across the plain. This was it: the way down, the door to the underworld. We descended.

There was the remnant of a cattle trail, and we followed it down, through cattails, past pools of green, rotten water. The water vanished into the earth; we were left with sand and tumbled stones. We crossed the skittery, neurotic tracks of mice and the paw prints of a lone coyote coming up the canyon to drink and then going down again.

The cliffs closed in on either side. Slick-rock chutes dropped in. We sloshed through deep sand, then crossed a floor of cracked bedrock. And then suddenly the canyon dropped off in a two-hundred-foot overhang; suddenly there was no place to go, no water in sight, and evening was coming on fast.

We consulted our map. It was unclear, but there was a suggestion of another side canyon entering the main canyon; perhaps we were in the wrong one. Mentally flipping a coin, we climbed out over the rimrock to the south and wandered across the naked sandstone, looking for another way down into the earth. The sun was falling fast, casting long shadows.

"What if we can't find a way down?" Susan asked.

"We'll sleep up here, I guess."

"But there's no water."

"Then we'll be thirsty." We were both getting a little worried, and a little cross. Danger on a quest is all right; discomfort, inconvenience, are not.

Finally we found another side canyon, a narrow notch dropping down almost like a trapdoor. Susan wasn't sure about it, but I slid into it and scrambled down a steep gulch that ended on a ledge high up on the cliffside of still another canyon. She joined me a few minutes later. The way looked difficult, but plausible. Besides, there was the fact of the map: someone had passed this way before.

We edged around a tight corner, a dizzying drop below, and found ourselves on a sloping ledge above another overhang. But this one led easily down to a crack, which we jammed. (Jamming a crack consists of forcing or angling your fists and feet into the crack, with sufficient pressure to keep you hanging there.)

The next ledge was even easier—a good thing, as we were both tired. Scrambling with heavy packs is gritty work, and Susan, though as light on her feet as a dancer, was built a little fine for that kind of slogging: it was like harnessing a thoroughbred to a plough. There was a catch in her breath, and her words trembled as if they might fall to pieces: she was all in.

The bottom of the canyon was lost in shadow; the sun was gone and the high rock walls above us had turned from blond to gold to bronze. The ledges wound down, somehow, miraculously; and then, luck on luck, we found the remains of the old pack trail we had missed, switchbacking in descent from the head of the canyon. This must have been the secret door, the gateway that that darkly shining woman had told me about in El Paso so long ago. A few minutes later we were coming out onto the canyon floor.

The last colors were fading on the cliffs; Venus was already lit, swinging like a lantern on the canyon rim. We walked down canyon, looking for a place to make camp. I remembered something Shohei Ooka had written in *Fires on the Plain*: "A thought struck me then with great force: I was walking along this path for the first time in my life, and yet I would never walk along it again." A man and a woman, half in love, wandering down a canyon at dusk, looking for water: there was something fine, something very old and fine, in that. Like Susan's best silver work, it was charged with the power of caring, and labor, and time.

We found a pool in sand just below a ledge—enough sand to spread two sleeping bags across and build a fire on. There was plenty of driftwood, reefs of it, sun-bleached logs and branches, washed down from the Abajo Mountains, caught against the cliffs. The water was clear as glass and had no smell, no taste.

A month or two earlier, in the flash-flood season, when the storm clouds roll off the Abajos, bruised and radium-bright, this would have been a fool spot to make camp. It could rain fifty miles away in the late afternoon, the slick rock would gather the runoff, and you would wake up in the middle of the night riding ten feet of water toward the San Juan River. But this was autumn: safe, or safe enough.

I gathered wood and built a fire. The logs, sucked dry and light as balsam by the sun, went up like gasoline with a single match. Sweet smell of cedar, piñon, aspen. We ate stew and airy chips of freeze-dried fruit, drank red wine and black tea. An owl called from down the canyon: a baleful cry, soft, spectral, meant to startle the mouse or hare from its cover. The full moon was rising somewhere over the edge of the earth. Moonlight, lunacy, descended the canyon wall, turning the rock to ice—hallucination of a glacier.

We had climbed down into another time, where it was easy to believe that an owl's cry meant death, that coyotes were tricksters, that weird bent mannikins called Mudmen lived at the bottom of the great rivers. Across the fire Susan combed the sand out of her hair and smiled that ancient, woman's smile at me. A different time, the past, where, they say, we must go to be reborn, to find our future, whatever it may be.

The next morning we packed up, broke camp and headed down canyon. It was a lukewarm sunny day.

Just as the El Paso stranger had said, there were Indian ruins everywhere in ledges and caves in the cliffs. About 9,000 years ago, paleo-Indian hunters and gatherers had filtered down into this canyon country and somehow learned to live hereabouts. Anything that was edible, they ate. That is how you survive in the desert—you become an extreme omnivore. These early desert people snared and netted rabbits and birds, and gathered and ground seeds, roots, berries. Insects and larvae were important sources of protein, as they are in all arid preagricultural societies. (The Australian aborigines treasure the wichetty grub, a fat, buttery larva they dig out of the ground and eat like a wriggling ice cream cone.) What few artifacts these desperate people had were breathtakingly beautiful in their craftsmanship: grinding stones, nets, basketry.

Thousands of years later, agriculture came north from Mexico, as did sorcery. Life was transformed: corn, beans and squash, the holy trinity of meso-America, gave the desert people a tighter, surer grasp on life. Crude pit houses and cave camps grew into towns, pueblos. *Anasazi* is a Navaho word meaning the old, or original, people; these Anasazis lived in the canyons of the San Juan until about 1200 AD, when they migrated south to New Mexico and northern Arizona, where their descendants, the Pueblo Indians, still live. This canyon country is just too friable, too fragile for long-term, intensive habitations. The Anasazis cut too much timber for roof beams, cleared too much brush for fields and just plain overbred. A cyclical drought may or may not have been the final disaster: archeologists, who reconstruct whole empires and civilizations out of the glaze on potsherds and discern the pattern of flakings on a spearpoint, disagree. It is too esoteric a point to do more than dream on: the Anasazis moved south, and that is that.

Hiking the canyon, we still felt the presence of those Old Ones. At one place on the cliff, we found hundreds of handprints in reddish paint, eerily like dried blood. You could still see the whorls in the fingerprints. On the Nile the fellahin place handprints on their walls to ward off the evil eye, djinns and demons. Was this cliff wall of hands a barrier against outsiders, spiritual or otherwise? Or was it a kind of simple codification of census, a symbolic counting up of the souls of a community? Some of the handprints were tiny, the hands of small children or infants. Below, in the ruins of a room, was a human pelvis, gleaming in the dust.

We trekked down canyon; the gods of the place were painted, scratched on the rocks. There was a feeling of being watched, a prickling at the back of the neck. The gods, demigods, spirits or whatever they were, were like the drawings of children or of the mad and they had that same inexplicable divinity to them—doodles, but fairly hissing with an arcane energy. Snakes, lightning, circles in circles in circles, arrows. That god from the far south of Mexico, a new-world Orpheus hunched over, playing a flute. And those tall, threatening isosceles figures with horns. Climbing up into the ruins of a kiva or a storehouse full of cobs of mummy corn, we felt like trespassers, invaders, ashamed.

Evening: miles down, the canyon walls went gray to delicate gold to roan to gray again. A wind came up the canyon, rippling the sand, jingling the yellow cottonwood leaves. We had come a long way that day: the canyon had turned and turned and turned again, till the map, with its side canyons and its springs and ruins, had lost all congruence with the country. It was a maze with canyon after cayon, ravine after ravine winding away into the rock.

We found a big clean pool, with a mud floor scrolled by worms, below a dried-up waterfall. We unpacked there, spreading our bags out on the sand. Susan had blood in one of her boots, from a blister: I cut and fixed a square of moleskin around it. And then we hauled logs and built a fire, a big one for light and joy as well as heat. Fire-building is easy in this tinder-dry country: you can get two fires from one match. The coals from the night's fire are still live the next morning, and you can lay twigs and bark across them and blow them ablaze.

The night came on. Above our heads the bats and moths danced their deadly dance in the light of the rising moon. Susan told me a long, long story about a train trip she once took in Brazil. She was madly in love with a jazz saxophonist from Rio, and the two of them made love all night long, so passionately loud that the other passengers complained and the conductors came at dawn and put them off the train at a tiny green town in the rain . . . "They do everything in rhythm there." She smiled at me. "The traffic moves, everyone walks in tune with the radios that are playing everywhere all the time. The whole country runs on music."

There was not another human being for forty, fifty miles. Far above, over the canyon rim, across the desolate mesa tops, a Piute rancheria, a Navaho sheep camp, a Mormon cowpoke reading by kerosene in a beat-up trailer. It was a precious feeling to be so alone: worth the sore feet, the sun-stung eyes, the muddy water we had to drink that looked like coffee and tasted like stone. The fire burned down; and in the last red light of the coals, I found myself looking at Susan and thinking of Deer Woman, the sensuous spirit in North American Indian tales who lures men off into the back country and steals their souls.

A coyote, a big gray one, scampered down canyon ahead of us in the cool of the next morning just as we started out; he stopped once, looked back over his shoulder at us, his eye full of a warm intelligence, and then bounded away through a stand of willow and was gone.

It is easy to come upon animals while hiking toward the river: the wind blows up from the San Juan, carrying sounds and smells before it, concealing the downwind traveler. Later that morning we surprised a giant porcupine perambulating away from a water hole, dragging his thousand quills—so big that at first we thought he was a black bear cub, wandered somehow down out of the mountains to the north. He clambered up into the rocks and then jammed himself into a crevice, quills out, hoping we would go away. We climbed up to get a good look at him: he rolled a tiny sorrowing eye back at us.

It was a good day for seeing animals and their signs. We found coyote, deer, raccoon tracks punched across the zinc mud of a dried-up pool. There was coyote scat everywhere: picking it apart, we found dry, wadded rabbit fur, husks of insects and berries, bluebird feathers, splinters of bone. Coyotes, like bears and men, will eat almost anything. Among the oddments found in coyote stomachs are horned toads, armadillo armor, bumblebees, rattlesnakes, centipedes, ropes, string, tire rubber, harness buckles, birds' eggs, honey and dirt. To a coyote the whole world is a banquet. No wonder the laugh that seems to lurk in that red, lolling mouth: it is a laugh of pure, unreasoning delight.

Pocket mice and lizards skittered into the dry brush, making a tremendous clatter way out of proportion to their size. Frogs bellowed from pools of copper-, coffee-, tobacco-colored water. High up in the cliffs were the mud pueblos of the canyon wren.

Sometimes you can walk for days in the wildest country and not see a sign of an animal. But this day was different for some reason. Who can tell why some days are swollen with significance and beauty, while so many are empty? My journal notes for the rest of that day record a whole series of encounters:

Marsh hawk dives at falling cottonwood leaf, not three feet from Susan's head—playing at a kill, or mistake? Strikes it from the air, and soars away.

Doe bounds away, stiff-legged; no other fresh tracks—a loner.

Big crow, glossy, vitreous, as if whittled out of bituminous coal, goes into a stall, drops down to look us over, caws an inscrutable *kroan,* floats away—impression of his intelligence, curiosity.

Evening, tired, looking for pueblos up in the cliffs, I almost step right on a rattler. Susan yells, I jump back. He is already coiled, tail whirring, flicking his black tongue. About ten inches long, a delicate pink and tan. Pygmy desert rat. Watch him till he edges away into the brush, and is gone. A great feeling of joy, at seeing him . . .

That night we camped below a fine ruin, turrets like a fortress, built along a series of alcoves in the cliff. Our camp was in a grove of huge, ancient cottonwood trees; the ground was yellow and sweet-smelling with fallen leaves going to duff.

I found myself thinking more and more about the Anasazi, the Old Ones, who had lived here and then moved on. It seemed to me that there was a secret, a message, wrapped up in their lives. They scratched farms out of the valley floor; built their aeries of riprap and mud; incised their gods and dreams on the cliffs; hunted deer, rabbit, desert bighorn; made baskets and pottery, lots of it, decorated with cord relief and colors of a smoldering barbaric beauty. Nothing special in that, perhaps: neolithic farmers living in tiny, simple communities that were little more than bands of a few extended families.

They were poor, if wealth can be measured in a society's energy and material available per capita. The garbage cans of any suburban American household probably hold more calories than the average Anasazi family got in a week. There was a kind of Taoist austerity to their lives; and yet, if their modern Pueblo descendants are any evidence of how they lived, they somehow squeezed a rich, sophisticated culture out of these fields of dust. Pueblo metaphysics—we would call it animism or magic—carried the theory of relativity into every corner and crevice of existence. You danced thunder out of the sky, rain out of the clouds, crops out of the earth. The bitter lightning in the rattlesnake speaks to the rain that gathers around the dark mountains. You bury your ancestors and they rise again as corn; turquoise embodies sky, abalone shell thunderhead, feathers wind and storm . . .

However it worked, it propelled the Anasazi way of life through drought, the raids of the Utes, Navahos and Comanches, and the imperial flexings of Spain and Anglo-America. It was a sinewy, enduring kind of poverty, indeed: it will probably outlast our petrochemical bubble of a republic by aeons.

We have contrived, as Marvin Harris and others have pointed out, a technology so abstruse that it takes us 3,000 calories of energy to produce a 300-calorie can of corn. The waters rise on Lake Powell, and silt drifts slowly against the dam at Page. The cities burn bright, stoked on the flesh of mountains and mesas and on the blood of rivers.

Some say that our complex systems contain the seeds of their own destruction; that like rapidly growing crystal lattices, they are brittle, unstable in proportion to their very size and rate of growth. They point out that those tiny gold-crazed gangs of Spaniards destroyed the urban Inca and Aztec empires in a matter of months, but that life in the tribal villages goes on undisturbed even today. And they claim that the Pueblo Indians will still be dancing their green-corn dances, and 'dobing their kiva walls, long after the last light in Los Angeles has gone out. Who knows? Not me.

Perhaps they are right, Lao-tze and Mao Tse-tung and Crazy Horse and all the rest. Perhaps less *is* more. Perhaps all that matters, all that lasts, is life close to the ground, down to the bedrock: village, pueblo, *ejidos,* sun-dance encampment; and all of our cities, our grand operas and coups, our fads and inventions, are just chaff in the wind.

Those were the kinds of thoughts we had, anyway, while putting logs on the fire, boiling up another billy of tea water as the clouds burned up like scraps of paper in the moon down that nameless, trailless canyon.

We went deeper, days, miles, into the earth.

Side canyons choked with alluvial stone and timber led off into nowhere. We crossed places out of a vision. Crackled geometry of dried mud; a bed of cobbles; a pool of worn-out water glowing like fire. Juniper trees, a forest of hags, knelt in the dusk; high up in a cliff that glistened like wet adobe we saw a stone turret with a dark window. Birds must have built it: there was no human way up there. Cottonwoods dropped their crisp gold drifts of leaf. Our tracks across the dunes were erased by the wind even as we looked back: it was as if we had never been there at all.

If there were any saints, any shamans or medicine men left, this was their kind of territory, far down the last canyon, atop the impassable butte, somewhere in the lost mountains between Hanksville and Sevier Dry Lake. That is the presence we felt, walking the canyon down to that distant river: invisible but always there, some naked, withered, centuries-old Anasazi cacique peering at us from his ledge, chanting a scrap of rain song, hawk song, beating time with a stick on a bighorn skull, as the New York–Los Angeles jet ploughed an icy furrow across the sky. Or was it all imagination?

The canyon narrowed; the sky shrank to a rivulet of blue. The last Indian signs faded out, vanished.

We entered a weird zone of fossil mud, petrified dunes, the cliff peeling off in iron-black blocks the size of battleships. There were walls of jackstrawed flood timber twenty feet high blocking the canyon floor; bones and stones and sticks and mud washed down from the world above, piled up in utter maniac confusion. Geology gone berserk.

There were desert bighorn there: we saw their tracks, like misshapen hearts, wherever there was water. But they were invisible in the smoky brush, in the mazeways of rock and rubble. And there were lions down there, the map said; but they flowed away like shadows into the lion-colored land, and left no traces.

We were in a place that was utterly lost. Its human history could have been written on a fingernail.

The Anasazis never tried to live this far into the canyon: too narrow, too rocky and decayed and . . . strange. The toughest Navaho couldn't run sheep through these scorched sepulchers.

Who had walked this canyon before us, other than that stranger from El Paso? Perhaps a lone Anasazi hunter, trailing a wounded bighorn; a band of wandering Utes; a Mormon cowboy, searching for stray range cattle; a greed-mad uranium prospector, looking for the mother lode to birth a million Hiroshimas . . . perhaps nobody. There was not a bootprint, not a scrap of paper, not a rusted can anywhere. It was as if we had fallen through the world of men, living and dead, into the benthic ooze of an America where nothing human had happened yet. We had slipped through the *sipapu,* the hole in the kiva's floor, the place of Emergence. It felt out of place, strange, to be human down there.

There were no signs except for the tracks in the sand where Porcupine had trudged along the canyon dragging his quills; and Coyote, of course, had been everywhere, looking for water, sniffing out food, checking things out with his boundless curiosity. There were deer prints, lots of them, by a spring where a side canyon led off, which the map called "Many Deer Canyon." Wrens flashed in the brush. A hummingbird whirred in the air, balanced on blurred wings; then vanished like a blown-out flame.

Descending a steep, narrow defile, we found a shiny chrome toad sitting inscrutable in the dry rubble. Susan bent down and picked him up, and suddenly he galvanized, kicked wildly, peed in her hand, jumped free and disappeared down a hole in the rocks. In a desolate gorge later that afternoon Susan found the wing feather of a desert hawk, zigzagged gray and white. She tied it in her hair, a talisman of that nameless, wordless wilderness.

It was hard country: nothing nice or comfortable about it. It was only gorgeous. There was just enough water left over from the late summer rains—here and there under rocks and in deep holes in the sand and mud—to keep us going. And it tasted bad, bitter as stone or sour with dead wood. The canyon floor became rougher and narrower, and now we were no longer hiking or walking, but actually *climbing* down the canyon: clambering up twenty-foot boulders, skidding down the other side, shinnying across walls of driftwood that shifted under our feet, then climbing more rocks. Up and down and up again. It was tough going with those big packs, especially for someone cut as close to the bone as Susan. She was a swift runner and a deft mover through the forest with a rifle or a stuff sack of osha roots slung over her shoulder; but hunched under a forty-pound pack, scrambling through the tumble stones at the bottom of this gorge, the raw red air tearing at her throat, she complained: "I guess I'm a mountain person. This country is just too broken up for me. It's just too *dry*. I'd like to see something green, my eye is dying for something green." Well, it was true: the greens of the piñon, sagebrush and juniper are all silver, or tarnished, or olive; the cottonwood was yellow, the Gambel's oak russet. It was not an easy landscape on the body or on the eye; but I loved it. It was *grand*—that was the word. How old were those layers of blond sea rock towering above us on either side? Unimaginable. You had to think in geologic time, just this side of astronomical time in terms of incredibility— 1.42 billion years ago? Somewhere above us in the rock that was so bright it seemed to luminesce were the bones of fish, birds, flying lizards and tiny horses that might have escaped from a fairy tale . . . and monsters slain and laid down in the benthos. The Buddhists and Hindus talk of time in *kotis* of *kalpas*: "As many grains of sand as there are in the Ganges, there are so many years in a single minute in one hour of Brahma's night, and his nights are endless . . ."

That was the kind of time we were descending with our heavy loads; and day after day, consulting the map (which we handled so much it threatened to come apart in our hands), we thought the river seemed no closer. Where the map said one mile, we had to travel two or three, cutting back and forth across the chaotic wash, bushwhacking along the steep talus slopes below the cliffs. *"Yossha,"* Susan kept exclaiming wearily: a word she picked up as a child in Japan that means "okay" or "all right" in every shade of meaning from delight to exhausted defeat—in this case, the latter. An all-purpose word, like the Hindi *a·cha*. It was awful going and it kept getting worse. The canyon steepened, as if it meant to carry us right down to the center of the earth in a series of ledges and rock chutes. The cliffs rose 2,000 feet on either side, streaked, broken by giant cones of talus, fallen walls, crumbled arches covered with twisted trees. Everything was broken down, suspended in the act of falling or shattered to pieces. We had to climb along gullies of loose rock high above the canyon floor; stones dislodged, bounced away, clattering down and off into space. The canyon turned and turned on itself again, like a snake in death there.

There is a stage in every quest, every journey, when you seem hopelessly suspended between where you were and where you are bound. That night, camped on a rickety ledge in a land of pure stone—no tree or bush in sight, only dry grass that looked as if it had died a hundred years ago, the chlorophyll burnt out of it—we felt like we were in the Land of the Dead. There was nothing to burn: we had a dark camp and cold food. Dry thunder rumbled somewhere off to the north. It sounded as if they were quarrying a sky of black marble, splitting it and letting the blocks tumble down. We were both weary beyond our limits, and a little bit unglued. A tear ran down Susan's face; when I tried to take her hand, she slapped me away: "I don't know why I came here! This is like hell. There's no river down here. It's a trick, you bastard!" For some reason that made me laugh; and then she was laughing too, and we embraced on our little stone-littered ledge overlooking desolation, with a sky of stone above. We laughed and laughed, holding each other; for there was a crazed, cracked beauty to it all—to the bad water, and the queasy trails that ended in mid-air, and the myth of a river that seemed to retreat, further and further, the more we walked; and the packs that felt like they were full of pig iron, and the sky as tight and dry as azure parchment. There is a beauty to such journeys that knocks logic to smithereens.

We went on down; there was no place else to go.

This was the beginning, the birthing place of the world, we felt. The air was thick with the smell of time, and silence lay heavy on the place. Days, frail skeletons of autumn cloud drifted across the narrow blue river of a sky above. The moon had waned, worn away. And we, we had turned hard and dark.

Only a hermit or a saint would live down there; and if you weren't mad when you arrived, you would be after a season or a year or two. We were already a little mad, a little out of step with our regular selves, after only—how long had it been? Ten days? Two weeks? We should have notched a stick, like Crusoe: but perhaps it was better to have left linear time behind and to fall back on the melting of the moon, the sun angling down toward winter . . .

We felt a subtle change; we had brought no watches or clocks with us, no heartless nickel ticking; and perhaps such things affect us more than we think. In his book *Parable of the Beast,* Bleibtreu has written, apropos of the effects of celestial cycles on human biochemistry (our modern version of the soul): "In some nearly hidden corner of our inner selves we are aware of happenings elsewhere in the solar system and perhaps in the universe at large." If so, perhaps the primitives who beat drums and clatter bells to frighten away an eclipse are wrong in a different way than we thought they were: they are venting a natural natal terror that we trap inside, where it sickens us. Perhaps there is an assonance between the human heartbeat, the sun, the moon and stars.

What if one were to stay down here outside the years? Susan and I talked about it while camped in a cave above a crescent pond of old, old water, water so old it tasted like excavated dust, fossil. What if we stayed down here just one season or half of a year? The technology of it would be easy. We would find a side canyon and rappel down three or four haul sacks of freeze-dried food: cache it in a south-facing cave well above the floodline, at a sunny place where two or three canyons converge, near a reliable spring; and plunder one of those drift-wood reefs for firewood. Weave a withy hut and nail it into the white sand with stones. Hunt the spooky canyon deer with a salt lick and rifle. Pick Mormon tea, drink the bitter, ephe-drinal brew, and stay up all night spinning yarns, knitting our own legends.

Would one learn anything down there? Someday, Susan said, the place might speak to you; drop its confounded reti-cence, its veils of illusion, and let you *know* something. You might hear a crow shout, and suddenly the rock would blaze with a pure, healing light. Or you might wake, after a night of restless dreaming, as a coyote: stare down at your body and see fire, ruffled gray fur, quick little paws, a bushy tail curled around to your nose, as you awake, sprawled in a new, keener world. Susan was always dreaming of the divine, a transfor-mation of some sudden kind: "Someday I'll work a piece of silver no one will believe: a piece that looks like it was made by magic." Though I wanted to, I couldn't believe her; at that time I thought all the great things were past, gone forever. The title mosaic in the sea-green roof of the mosque at Mazar-i-Sharif; the gold-in-bronze metallurgy of the Shan dynasty: the *Gold-berg Variations;* the corn dance. Who, in this shabby, latter-day Iron Age, could create anything of that quality? We are lucky to have relics from these early divine times, I thought; now I am not so sure.

And then one dusk we turned a final corner; and there below, beyond white dunes and willows, was the lost river, the San Juan, flowing like light through its gorge. In a dusk the color of roses we walked the last steps down to the water that for so long had been a mystery, an empty promise, up in those dry cascades of rock. The "El Paso stranger" and her map had been right—there *was* a way down to the river.

Everything seems lost in the desert. There always seems to be another twist in the canyon wall, another crook in the cliff. Gods sing to you and then drop down a trap door into the past.

Water slithers away like silk and is gone. The answer slips through your fingers like sand; the old prospector always dies before he can tell you the way to the Lost Dutchman. You call out for help and get an echo back. You walk, and dream, and walk some more, till your feet bleed and your tongue turns black. Maybe you find what you are looking for, maybe you don't. But all journeys in the desert are pilgrimages: you come out wiser, with some of the cheap shine worn off.

We made camp on the lost beach. Across the river the northernmost cliffs of the Navaho Nation bled in the last light. An eagle shrieked, hunting high, high over the water to the west. We unrolled our bags and built a bonfire of logs washed down from the faraway mountains: big logs, screw pine and fir, from high up in the snow country. Our food was running low; but we made a great feast of bulghur, the last two cans of turkey and the bottle of champagne we had packed all the way down here. We still had a long, long way to go, to ever get out: east, the map said, on a sketchy track high above the river, and then north through unknown country, more mazes of canyon. But we could not think of that. We were, for the time being, home.

The river of old snow, thick with stone and sand and soil, rolled by in the last light, jade. In the old days you could have ridden it all the way down to the sea; now, somewhere below, the Colorado and the San Juan backed up, dammed. Not a drop reaches the Sea of Cortez, and the old delta is a necrotic, etiolated place of salts, ghosts, mummified creeks and inlets. Someday I would have to go there and see.

Fire burst from those big river logs. Night came on.

Lying there, listening to that vast water that after all those days of still aridity sounded like a million wet, white wings beating a heavy sky, we might have been the only people on the face of the earth.

Days later, we were walking across a mesa at sunset, trying to find Susan's truck. Our food and water were gone; Susan was sobbing and cursing me; I slogged on, head down, morose: pilgrims on their way home. The sky was vast again. Far, far away in the four directions, sacred mountains nailed down the corners of the earth. We trudged along through the orange sand. The sagebrush looked gray as cigarette ash. The land appeared flat, unbroken, where we had been: there was no sign at all of a canyon or a river. It was gone, all gone, as if we had only imagined it and then snapped back to reality; except for the hawk's feather, like a tiny strip of lightning, shining there in Susan's hair.

The
Colorado
Plateau

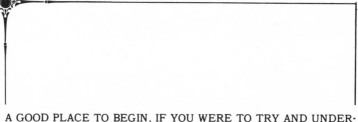

A GOOD PLACE TO BEGIN, IF YOU WERE TO TRY AND UNDER-
stand something of the Colorado Plateau, is Zuñi Pueblo. Zuñi
lies on the river of the same name, in the hilly country south of
Gallup, New Mexico. The Zuñi River flows into the Little
Colorado near the Petrified Forest; the Little Colorado enters
the Colorado itself just south of Marble Gorge.

When the Spanish came to Zuñi (they called the place the
Cities of Hawikuh) back in the seventeenth century, they tried
to convert the Indians to Catholicism. A priest challenged the
magicians of Zuñi to a contest: if the Catholic god proved to
have greater powers than the Zuñi god, the Zuñis would give
up their old religion; if not, the Spanish would leave the Zuñis
alone.

After an inconclusive series of trials, the sly priest produced
a flintlock musket, pointed it at a tree a hundred feet away and,
as the Zuñis stood watching, took aim and fired, knocking a
branch from the tree. "Our god can do that," the priest said,
conveniently ignoring the fact that gunpowder had been in-
vented by a bunch of Taoist alchemists in China.

"H'm," said the head Zuñi magician. He brought out a chunk
of rock called a thunder flint, muttered an incantation and
pointed it at the tree. The tree exploded into pieces, leaving
nothing but a cloud of smoke and a few shreds of bark. So
much for Catholicism at Zuñi.

Every winter Zuñis hold a dance called Shalako. Shalakos
are tall, conical figures ten feet high, garishly colored, hung
with feathers, topped with huge goggle-eyed masks with long
clacking beaks. They look like nothing else in the world. They
are totally unfamiliar. Wherever they came from, it was far, far
away and very, very strange.

On the evening of the Shalako dance, these holy gro-
tesques come dancing down out of the mountains, six of them,

into the pueblo. They make their way to six ceremonial houses scattered throughout the town, where, along with masked gods like Hututu, Shulawitsi, Sayatasha and the Koyemshi, or Mudmen, they dance through the long, cold night. To go to a Shalako is to be suddenly plunged back into the golden age of the Neolithic. The pueblo is packed with Indians, Zuñis, visitors from other pueblos, Navahos. The night is alive with the heartbeat of drums, the low, fierce chanting of massed voices. Gods with horns, gaudy red gods, Mudmen from the floor of the Colorado River, appear dancing in the night and vanish again like apparitions.

No one really knows what "Shalako" means except the Zuñis, and they aren't talking—or rather, they tell so many different stories that you end up knowing less than you did before. Shalako is a hunting dance. Shalako is a dance of the dead. Shalako is a history of the Zuñi universe, a fertility rite, an honoring of the mountain spirits, an invocation of nameless energies . . .

But what it means is not so important as the fact that it *works*: something inexplicable, wonderful, really does happen on those dark, snowy nights of dancing. An anthropologist friend who had worked in the Zuñi area for years took a young couple from Finland to a Shalako one winter. They sat in one of the six ceremonial houses, watching the tall god swoop back and forth. Ti e night wore on and on; sometime in the middle of the night, the Finnish woman decided she needed some fresh air; she squeezed her way out through the stifling crowds. A few minutes later she came back in and found that a big Navaho man blocked the way back to her seat. She whispered across to her husband in Finnish, "Where should I sit?" Suddenly (both she and her husband swore this really happened) the Shalako stopped dead in its dance and turned to them, and a voice from under the mask said in perfect Finnish, "Sit behind that big fat Navaho." The rest of the night, the couple sat watching the dancing in a state of shock. Just before dawn, as the dancing was about to end, the Shalako and five or six of the other masked gods lined up and, again in perfect Finnish, chanted to the beat of the drum, "Have a very, very unmerry Christmas! Have a very, very unmerry Christmas!"

I went to Shalako once, several years ago. It was twenty below zero that night, and toward dawn it began to snow. I stood outside one of the six ritual houses, frozen numb, my feet aching in their boots, peering in through the window at the dancing gods. It was a powerful night. I didn't understand what was happening, but I *felt* it. Like any very old ritual—a High Latin Mass, a Tibetan Buddhist *puja,* a Greek play—it needed no reason. It was a slow, majestic unveiling of ancient potencies, and it stirred me in ways I can't describe.

The only time I really *met* a Zuñi Indian was in Flagstaff, at the Fourth of July Pow-wow, about ten years ago. I was eating Chinese food at the railroad café. The place was jammed with Indians, most of them four shots over the line and getting worse fast. A Zuñi guy with a pint of peach brandy in his hip pocket sat down in my booth and asked me for a couple of bucks. "No way," I said. "Want to buy a necklace?" he asked, producing a string of fake-looking heishi beads. "No thanks," I said. Then he offered to teach me "a sacred Zuñi song" for two dollars. Ignoring my protests, he stood up and began to do a stomp dance beside the booth, chanting, "Hey ya ay ya na, hey ya ay ya na!" I got up to go to the men's room to escape him; I was standing at the urinal when he came dancing in, still singing, his palm out: "Hey ya ay ya na na, hey ya ay ya na!" "No," I said. He stopped. Then his face lit up. "How about a different song?" he asked, and began chanting again, before I could stop him: "Hey ya ya hey ya ya yana, yana yana—"

I walked out through the café and onto the sidewalk; when I looked back in the window, the Zuñi had sat down at my booth and was wolfing down the rest of my egg foo yung.

I traveled the Colorado Plateau country for nearly a decade, from the stone country the Utes called *Toom'pin wunear'*

Tuweap', or Rock Land—around the Grabens, the Paradox Formation and Cigarette Springs in Utah—down to Zuñi Pueblo, Navaho Mountain and Sacred Mountain Trading Post in Arizona. I never really figured the country out. I traveled the plateau doggedly, persistently, like one of those old-time Indians who would walk and walk and walk across the country till he found a vision. The problem was, visions were all too easy to find out there in the plateau: they were everywhere, riddling the solid world with their gnostic fires. Visions rolled down the night highways; they reared in the timber at night on Cottonwood Pass; they rippled on the still waters in the chasms, in the dim liturgy of the squawfish, in canyons like Desha, Fish, Dark. Castaneda has written of "power places" in his books; well, sometimes the whole plateau seemed like one big power place to me, carved out of a single titanic loadstone, every river a Styx or Olph, every pebble in the trail a Rosetta stone.

The Jivaro Indians of the Amazon believe that the waking world is an illusion, insubstantial, and that ultimately only dreams and visions are real. They drink a hallucinogenic decoction called *yage* or *ayahuasca,* and dream long journeys across imaginary continents; journeys which seem, in the drugged, alkaloidal slumbers, to last weeks, even months. Jivaro shamans have even drawn maps of this mental landscape, showing its mountains, rivers and lakes. At least your dream cannot be defoliated, burned, cut to pieces and hauled away. Or so I used to think; now I am not so sure.

Who really knew the plateau? The early explorers were so strung out on gold and silver that the land curdled into thin-air treasure before their eyes. The Indians found that they could get rid of the Spanish by telling them that there were gold and silver just over the horizon to the north: the Seven Golden Cities of Cibola, where even the houses and streets were hammered out of pure gold; at dusk, it was said, the natives rang bells of gold and silver. That was the kind of music the Spanish liked the best—a precious-metals rumba—and they followed this delusion a long, long way. In 1540, Coronado and his men made it all the way to the south rim of the Grand Canyon; in

1776, Escalante and Miera reached the Uinta River in what is now northern Utah, and the dread Great Basin country around Sevier Lake.

These were epic, heroic journeys. Horses were sucked under by quicksand. Starving men survived on cactus with the spines burned off, and piñon nuts. None of the early explorers really knew where they were. Lost in the Great Salt Lake country of Utah in 1776, Miera, the cartographer of the Escalante expedition, insisted that Monterey, California, was only a week away over the mountains to the west!

There is something at once hilarious, pathetic and awful about these crossed men trudging through endless wastelands, coming upon a lone brush wickiup in the middle of nowhere and asking the Indian who squatted inside like an emaciated Buddha, "Ah, where do you keep the golden bells around this place?" Just look at a map of the Escalante expedition: They left Santa Fe on July 29, 1776; traveled northwest across badlands and desert into the Rockies; followed the gorge of the Dolores River from present-day Dolores to the mesa country along the Utah border; crossed the San Juan Mountains, backtracking to the northeast; traversed the Colorado Rockies south to north, turning west and arriving in the Provo area around September 20; traveled south and then east again, through Pipe Springs and Kaibab, crossing the Colorado River north of Page, visiting the Hopi mesas and Zuñi and returning to Santa Fe on January 2, 1777. Madness.

No one ever found the Seven Golden Cities of Cibola, but many kept right on looking. In the nineteenth century a new version of the myth appeared: America west of the 100th meridian, the myth said, was a Garden of Eden in disguise; if you cut through the hard crust of the Great Plains with a plough, moisture would pour out like the steam from a plum pudding; the sky would fill with clouds, rain would fall and the plains would become green, fertile farmland. The Colorado River and its tributaries, the fantasy went on, were great potential trade routes, easily navigable, and the stony mesas surrounding them were covered with golden humus.

In pursuit of this pipe dream, a certain Captain Samuel Adams decided to navigate the Colorado River from Breckenridge, Colorado, 9,000 feet up in the Rockies, to the Sea of Cortez—something like trying to build a highway from Nepal to Tibet right over the summit of Everest. Adams and his men set off down the Blue River, a rocky, rough little alpine stream, on July 12, 1868. One month, four lost boats and less than a hundred miles later, they gave up. Adams declared his expedition a complete success: the worst part of the river, he said, had been run, and the way to the sea was open!

About the same time as Adams's quixotic journey, John Wesley Powell was running the Colorado River from Flaming Gorge in Wyoming all the way through Cataract and Grand canyons. Powell's journey took ninety-five days. Boats were smashed to pieces in the rapids, and three of the ten expedition members deserted and were killed by Shivwits Indians on the canyon rim.

Powell's account of the trip, *The Exploration of the Colorado River and Its Canyons,* undid forever the myth of a rich and easy Colorado Plateau. But at the same time it revealed the real greatness of the Colorado: its mystery, its gorgeous difficulty. No one would ever strike it rich out there, but they would be constantly amazed. "And what a world of grandeur is spread before us!" Powell wrote of the country around the confluence of the Green and Colorado rivers. "Between us and the distant cliffs are the strangely carved and pinnacled rocks of the *Toom'pin wunear' Tuweap'.* On the summit of the opposite wall of the canyon are rock forms that we do not understand ... Wherever we look there is but a wilderness of rocks—deep gorges where the rivers are lost below cliffs and towers and pinnacles, and ten thousand strangely carved forms in every direction, and beyond them mountains blending with the clouds."

There is a Japanese sport, called *sawanabori,* in which you follow streams to their origins. The Japanese writer Tsunemichi Ikeda describes it this way: "Climbers sometimes walk in the streams or climb the side wall of the waterfalls . . . The origin of *sawanabori* is said to be the shortcuts of hunters in the old days."

Sawanabori is a fine way to explore the smaller peripheral canyons of the Colorado: places like Grand Gulch, Canyon del Muerto and Canyon de Chelly, Owl, Fish, Desha, Nasja and Horse canyons and all the rest, and the weird, embrangled places like Ernie's Country, the Grabens, the Needles, the Maze, and Behind-the-Rocks. There isn't enough water in the side canyons to float, but usually there is enough so you won't die of thirst. *Sawanabori* is not only a sport, it is a kind of ritual, like many ancient games: a pilgrimage along the natural pathways of free-running water. In the desert the ritual has a more intense kind of beauty; following water is the holiest kind of quest in a dry land. Even sophisticated, abstract gods like Allah and Yahweh can't escape their desert past: they appear in a clap of thunder with a flash of lightning, cloaked in life-giving rain. Their holy places are oases, rivers, cloud-covered mountains.

There is a painting by Paul Klee called, I believe, "Secret Door": a gray, stony chasm with glowing arrows pointing the way down to a luminous opening deep in the rocks. Klee never visited the Colorado Plateau, of course, but his archetypal image, as simple and striking as an Anasazi glyph, evokes precisely that reclusive country, its labyrinthine mysteries.

One autumn day, hiking a nameless canyon in the Needles country of Utah, I decided to try and follow a vague passageway up through the slick-rock canyon walls. The Needles are one of the oddest pieces of geography in the plateau: they are part of the "ten thousand strangely carved forms" Powell described, the solid-rock land east of the confluence of the Green and Colorado rivers. Sandstone pagodas lean in drunken clusters; crooked gorges called grabens, formed by the collapse of salt beds deep in the bedrock, coil on and on, leading you in

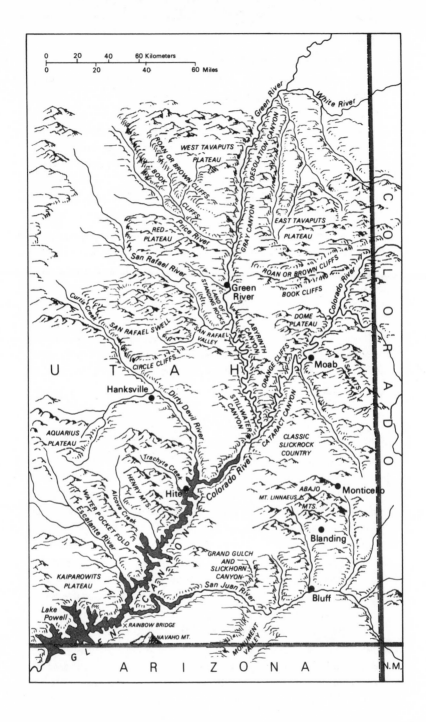

circles. A giant's foot of red eroded stone is silhouetted against the sky. To the east the North and South Sixshooter peaks point skyward, looking like their names. It is a child's idea of the desert, a landscape studded with naïve, primeval images: geology by Disney.

I clambered up the slick rock, following a tenuous crack system. Traveling across slick rock is something between climbing, scrambling and delicate walking: you tiptoe up, pressing your fingertips against the stone for balance, until the gradient becomes too steep and you have to pull yourself up, using nubbins and hollows for handholds. The rock rolls away in every direction, a steep, smooth sea of reds, grays, bone-whites. It is a graceful realm that almost forces you to move with grace.

As I moved up through the slick rock, my shadow stretched out long and lithe in the slanting sun; the crack widened to a crevice. An elegant black ribbon of old water raveled down the gilded stone. I emerged into a kind of miniature amphitheater in the canyon wall; in its center was a *tinaja,* a natural tank of old water ten or twelve feet deep, cold and clear as diamond. No one had ever been in that place before; I was the first; I could feel it in my bones.

Looking back to the east, I could see a hundred miles to the snow-covered La Sals just south of Moab, invisible over the curve of the earth. To the southeast, jumbled rouge stone, the dark, slate-colored mass of the Abajos beyond, far away. A pair of blue herons flew slowly down the canyon below, apparitions the color of the ocean.

There were no tracks in the fine dry sand around the edges of the pool; only the delicate circles around each tuft of desert grass, drawn by the tips of the blades turning in the wind.

There is a peculiar feeling to places without histories. In a sense this tiny hanging world was born when I crawled up into it from the canyon below: this was the first hour, day one, of creation. In another sense, I was never there.

I watched the sunlight fade over the world below; then, as dusk came on, I began to work my way north across the slick rock—the way I had come up was too steep to down-climb.

The slick rock went on and on. It got dark; there was only the dimmest kind of starlight. I followed wrong-way gullies, came to impassable overhangs, backtracked blindly into the rocks. I spooked something, a coyote, that uttered a harsh exhalation of surprise and scampered away: I heard claws clash on stone, a sound like tiny dull knives whittling away at something very hard.

Finally, after some hours I came out onto a kind of promontory, and in the distance of the immense night, I could see the tiny lights of the campground at Squaw Flats. A faint, pale scar of a trail led down through the rocks . . .

Secret doors: there are so many of them out on the Colorado Plateau. Secret doors to other, lost worlds, spinning their own time, turning on their own occult axes. As I crossed the famished mesa country west of Cigarette Springs on a bad, bad road one night, a bitter green smell penetrated my nostrils. I stopped the car, got out and followed the smell across a hundred yards of dust and dry rocks to find a *lake.* There were cattails higher than my head and, as I walked around the shore to the west, a small forest of cottonwood and cedar. The air was full of the silver, rippling music of water and the electric whir of insects. An owl called from off in the trees.

How could there be a lake four miles north of Hat Rock on Hardscrabble Mesa? Where does the water come from? And why doesn't the sun drink it up on that barren rock mesa top? After a while, one despairs of ever answering such questions. There are things that are, and they obey their own obdurate laws on the plateau.

Thirty-odd miles south of where I live is a pass called Lizard Head, between Sheep Mountain and the Wilson Peaks. Lizard Head divides the drainages of the San Miguel River, which flows north past Telluride, and of the Dolores, or the Rio Doloroso, which flows south off Lizard Head.

The Dolores is one of the great illogical rivers of the world; it does everything but run uphill. First it flows south out of the San Juan Mountains for about seventy miles; if it had any sense of what is right, it would keep on going down through the valley between Mesa Verde and Sleeping Ute Mountain, and join the San Juan River at Shiprock. Instead, the Dolores doubles back to the northeast just where it leaves the mountains—at the town of Dolores—cutting a deep gorge across a hundred miles of high, wild mesas. At the town of Bedrock, the Dolores leaves its gorge and crosses the Paradox Valley. More strangeness: the Paradox got its name because it *looks* like a classic Southwestern river valley—high sandstone cliffs on both sides, green bottomlands—but there is no river in it, only the Dolores crossing it at *right angles* and vanishing into its gorge again on the north side of the valley! The geology of all this is bizarre: the Paradox Valley formed when a salt bed (appropriately called the Paradox Formation) hundreds of feet thick collapsed, bringing the sandstone on top down with it. Anyhow, the Dolores keeps running north by northwest seventy more miles, till it hits the Colorado River just over the border in Utah between Moab and Cisco, in a crenellated rock country that is classic *Toom'pin wunear' Tuweap'*.

The Dolores sums up a lot of things about the Colorado Plateau: paradox, wildness and, most important of all, the fragility of life. The whole Colorado Plateau drainage, which waters Los Angeles, the great agricultural valleys of southern California, the desert cities of Arizona—between 13 and 17 million acre-feet of water a year—depends on quirky little rivers like the Dolores, the Animas, the Dirty Devil, the Pariah. Perhaps three quarters of the water those rivers feed into the Colorado is snowmelt. The Rockies, where the Colorado River gets its water, are really arid mountains; if you took away the winter snows, they would look like the Hindu Kush in Afghanistan—barren, almost treeless. Life in places like LA, then, depends on how much snow falls in the Rockies in a given winter. Anyone who lives in Los Angeles should go to Bedrock, Colorado, in the late spring, toward the end of the runoff season. You can sit there by the Highway 90 bridge and watch the Dolores fall. One week the raft and kayak season is at its height: boats are staving in on rapids like Snaggletooth and the Wall; a brown flood tide thick with timber, stones and mud roars by, hell-bent for its confluence with the Colorado. Two weeks later you can ride a horse right up the riverbed all the way to Slickrock, four to six miles upstream. You may have to wade a few sections and dodge some remnant pools, but you can do it.

Where the Dolores River crosses the far west end of San Miguel County, out toward the La Sal Mountains of Utah, is some of the most primitive country on the Colorado Plateau. There are only two towns out there: Egnar ("range" spelled backward), where they raise pinto beans (Dove Creek, to the south, is the self-proclaimed Pinto Bean Capital of the World); and Slickrock, little more than a general store, café and gas station for the ranchers and uranium miners who live out in Dry Creek Basin, Big and Little Gypsum valleys, places like that.

No one will ever get rich selling postcards of the West End. Large stretches of it consist of stucco-colored buttes, collapsing here and there into piles of stucco-colored rock debris. Dry, empty valleys lead to other dry, empty valleys, and the abandoned corpse of a pickup truck by the road has the impact of a monument. It's the real Old West out there, warts and all. Once in a long while, a news story makes it out of the West End into the pages of the county's only newspaper, the *Telluride Times*. When it does, it usually seems to be a story about cattle rustling or another incident—a trespassing, a shooting—in some long-standing land feud. "I told the sheriff," I heard one old West End lone-wolf miner say once, "that if I caught him sneakin' on my land one more time, I'd fill him with so much lead they'd have to use a back hoe to haul the body away!" They still mine the old way in the West End, one or two miners working a claim in some far-off gulch, doing all the blasting, timbering and assay work themselves, hauling the yellowcake out in a busted-up ore truck with no license plates and no brakes. Sometimes they come wandering into the Slickrock store to pick up supplies and mail—drenched in radioactive dust, looking like they just burrowed in from Bedlam, with angry, loco eyes glaring, seeming not of this century, this world, at all. Many of the West Enders are Mormons, immigrants from Utah. There are wandering hard-rock miners, following rumors of lodes and strikes across the West, and a few Navahos. They still hunt bears somewhere up in those cliffs. It's hard to see how bears could live in that stony scrub-timber country, but they do. They come down into the ranches and kill calves and sheep; and then the ranchers ride up into the hills, track them down and shoot them. They eat the bear meat.

"I don't know where the bears all come from," a young West End ranch hand told me once. "We kill four or five every year, and every year it seems like there's more than before. I guess there's always been bears here, and there always will be."

I thought about that—where the bears come from—and I decided, after a while, that they came from someplace off the map, somewhere invisible. René Daumal, the French mountaineer and Symbolist poet, wrote a terrific little book called *Mount Analog,* in which he postulated a mountain higher than Everest, a mountain on the border between myth and reality, physics and metaphysics. Daumal died of tuberculosis before he could complete the book; it ends in mid-sentence, in fact. But it is a lovely idea. That must be where the bears come from: a desert Mount Analog, with its own canyons, rivers, mesas, out there somewhere.

Two summers ago, on June 21, the day of the summer solstice, five of us sat around a campfire on a beach deep in the Serpentine Canyon of the Dolores and talked about the plateau country. We had rafted twenty-four miles of the river that day, down from Big Gypsum Valley. It was a high-water spring: usually the Dolores is too low for rafting by late June, but only a week ago this same raft, with a different crew, had crashed on Snaggletooth, the largest rapid on the Dolores, and torn a three-foot-long hole in the floor.

The river rolled by in the late afternoon, riffling over gravel bars and shoals. The air was still hot; the tall canyon walls, shining with panes of black desert varnish as tall as a skyscraper, radiated the heat of the long solstice day. Sitting on driftwood logs on the sand, listening to the coffee rumble on the Coleman stove, we traded stories about the Colorado River country.

Someone had been running the rapids in Cataract Canyon, on the Colorado River between its confluence with the Green River and Lake Powell. The rapids were tough, at least a seven (white-water rafters rate rapids on a scale from one to ten, ten being the almost impossible). Just as they were entering a particularly tough stretch of water, someone saw a coyote swimming down the rapids ahead of them. At first they thought the animal was crazy or dying or something; but the coyote led them right through the rapids, swam to the left bank of the river, trotted up onto a sand bar and watched them go by. That reminded somebody of Georgie Clark. Georgie has been leading white-water expeditions on the Colorado since 1944. In the spring of 1945 she persuaded a friend to float the Colorado River with her in life preservers. They jumped in the river at Peach Springs, with a tin of candy, some powdered coffee and dried soup their only supplies; it took them three days to float the sixty miles to Lake Mead, through tremendous rapids and whirlpools.

Someone else was kayaking the Grand when they met a lone Hopi Indian man on a beach where the Little Colorado flows into the canyon. The Hopi's face was painted black. "I'm waiting here for a vision," he told the kayaker, "but you're not it."

Someone else had found the Hopi Sipapu, the travertine spring in a side canyon of the Colorado where, the Hopis believe, they and the other beings who populate this world emerged from the last world. It was a weird place, a steaming cone with painted prayer sticks planted around the hole. One bold (or foolish) fellow in the party decided he wanted to climb down and see what the last world looked like. They lowered him down on a rope. "How is it down there?" they called. There was no answer. When they pulled him up, he was unconscious. He came to a few minutes later and told them it was dark in the last world, and you couldn't breathe the air.

There were a lot of good places in the Colorado Plateau, everyone agreed: the Henry Mountains, the last mountain range in the United States south of Alaska to be mapped; the Maze, on the far side of the Colorado just south of the confluence, as remote as the dark side of the moon; Horseshoe Canyon, west of the Labyrinth Canyon of the Green River . . . places none of us had been yet, enough places to last a lifetime . . .

They are going to build a dam on the Dolores. The project has made it through Congress, past the environmental lawsuits: it is an undeniable reality. The dam would drown the old McPhee Ranch below the town of Dolores; the impounded water would be pumped up onto the mesas to the south, for the pinto bean farmers and the land speculators.

No one was sure if there would be any river-running on the Dolores after the dam; they might not let enough water through to the lower river. One thing seemed sure: the great, wild floods of the spring runoff would be gone forever.

Twilight in the canyon: beauty with a keen edge of sorrow. Canyon wrens dove through the cooling air, over the gray and golden waters. There would never be another evening like this, ever again, in all our lives.

Navaho Mountain

IF THE LANDSCAPE OF THE COLORADO PLATEAU IS AN END-less series of monkey puzzles in stone, the people who live out there are an enigmatic bunch too: The Mormons, in their all-American angel-possessed Zion. The implacable Utes of Sleeping Ute Mountain, who believe that their mountain is a giant Indian who one day will awaken, rise up and chase the white man out of southwestern Colorado. Basque sheepherd-ers. Mexican hard-rock silver miners. Desert rats, uranium wildcatters, true-grit ranchers. And, strangest of all, the Na-vahos; or, as they prefer to be called, *Dineh,* meaning the Peo-ple, as opposed to all the lesser peoples of the world. The Navahos occupy almost the entire southern third of the Color-ado Plateau, an area as big as New England, from Albuquer-que in the east to the Grand Canyon in the west, from the San Juan River in the north to Gallup and Flagstaff in the south. *Dinetah,* the land of the People, is 25,000 square miles of rain-bow-colored, poverty-stricken wasteland, a Neolithic nation-state in the middle of modern America.

I first scraped the edge of the Navaho world back in the early seventies, when I was still living in Denver. I was working as an anthropologist, and one of my first research projects was a study of Navaho immigrants in the Denver area. The Bureau of Indian Affairs was trying to get Navahos to leave the reserva-tion and move to the city—"relocation," it was called—and Denver was a favorite relocation city. The relocatees, almost all of them from tiny rural communities like Cornfields, Bitter Water, Nazlini, Tez Nez Iah, were trained in such bottom-dog occupations as hairdressing, auto upholstering, dishwashing and the like, and turned loose on the lower reaches of the urban job market. Meanwhile, big Anglo energy companies were moving onto the Navaho reservation, building generating plants, mining coal and uranium, drilling for oil and hiring

Anglos to do most of the work. No wonder most Navahos viewed relocation as just another installment in the white man's genocidal schemes.

The pride of the Denver relocation program was a Navaho man in his mid-forties, with a wife and several children, who had moved to Denver in the sixties and stayed on for several years. He had a high-paying construction job and a house in the suburbs. One day, without warning, he put his house up for sale, quit his job and announced he was moving back to the reservation. The Denver BIA officials couldn't believe it. "Oh, I always hated it here," the Navaho told them. "There are just too many Anglos; they make me nervous. Now I've saved enough money to buy me a big herd of sheep and goats, and I'm going home to be a sheepherder." You can take a Dineh out of Dinetah, but you can't take the Dinetah out of the Dineh.

Every Friday and Saturday night you could find most of the Denver Navaho community at a bar I will call the Cowboy and Indian, a rough-and-trouble joint near the Colfax strip, the honky-tonk section of the city. There were other Indian bars in Denver—the Sioux and the other northern Great Plains tribes drank mostly at a dangerous, bucket-of-blood place in another part of town—but the Cowboy and Indian was the real core of Navaho life in Denver, a kind of ongoing alcoholic pow-wow. When a Navaho came up from the reservation, it was the first place he headed for; there he could pick up the gossip on the Indian grapevine, make friends (and enemies and lovers) and, of course, drink.

It was a red-hot place, with a feverish sheen. There were three bouncers, a big, big-bellied Cheyenne ex-prize fighter named Thompson and two quiet, sinister Anglos, one armed with a heavy police flashlight, the other with a revolver. The jukebox blasted country-and-western music, the floor was crowded with dancing couples swinging each other around; the ceiling rolled with smoke, and there was hard laughter and loud talk, Navaho and English: "I come up from Teec Nos Pos to fin' my cousin, he said he could get me a job on a loading dock, but now he's down in Santa Fe . . ." "Hey, I was in Khe

Sanh same time you was; tha's where I picked up this shrapnel
in ma hand . . ." "Buy us a round. Don't act like a sour-faced
Anglo . . ."

The drinking at the Cowboy and Indian was anesthetic, an-
algesic, curiously unjoyous; one got the feeling that most of the
drinkers would have been just as happy if someone hit them
between the eyes with a rubber mallet or etherized them.
Numbness was the name of the game. The Denver Navahos
were exiles, DPs, and they drank to ward off the loneliness, the
fear. Occasionally, in the sick, small hours of a Saturday night,
you would hear a scrap of a holy song—"Beautyway" or "Coyo-
teway" or "Shootingstarway," one of the great traditional rituals of the Dineh—sung over the drunken babble by some
whiskeyed-up soul. It was beautiful, and awful.

The first time I went down to the Navaho reservation, driving
south from Cortez, Colorado, the country struck me with the
force of a foreign land: Mongolia during the reign of the Khans
or eighteenth-century Afghanistan, perhaps. The men looked
like Central Asian cowboys (later, in Tibetan refugee camps in
India, I would see the same faces): flat, cuprous, epicanthic
faces, many with long hair topped by incongruous felt Stet-
sons. Many of the women wore long satin dresses and shining
velveteen blouses; they looked like desert princesses (and, in a
way, perhaps they are). Off in the sagebrush were the beehive-
shaped houses called hogans—built out of timber, planks, solid
adobe—that Navahos believe are the only proper dwellings
under the sun.

Driving south to Shiprock and then west to Kayenta that
first day on the reservation, I found I had entered a whole other
cognitive universe; everything was different. Vast deserts of
sage swept away to distant surreal mountains. An old Buddha-
faced man walked away across the dunes, driving a herd of
goats before him. Turquoise pickup trucks rolled down the
endless highways. I heard a Navaho talking about the Bible on
the car radio. "Jesus was a Navaho," I thought I heard him say.

In a café near Teec Nos Pos I ate something called a Navaho taco: ground beef, chili sauce, onions and cheese, on a heavy slab of Indian fry bread. The café was full of big Indians in tall twenty-gallon hats. Two girls came in and ordered coffee. They began to talk in Navaho, a language that manages to sound both slurred and bitten off at the same time. Every once in a while, an English word would pop up in the soft stream of Athabascan*: "basketball game," "Chevy pickup," "cheese-burger." One of the girls went over to the jukebox, put in a quarter and punched three songs: "Okie From Muskogee," "Purple Haze" and "Wasted Days and Wasted Nights," by Freddy Fender. Later that afternoon I picked up a hitch-hiker, a kid on his way home to Kayenta: "My cousins and I started a rock-'n'-roll band," he told me. "We were doing great till Marvin got scared by witches and got sick."

I had traveled down to the Navaho Nation to study some-thing called "acculturation, education and social adjustment"; but it seemed like something much stranger, and more won-derful, was happening. It was as if you sat down to study German irregular verbs, and suddenly a mad message in fire leapt out of the gray grammar, astounding you.

Anglo geographers rate a fifth of the Navaho land base as totally useless for farming or grazing, and another 50 percent as only poor to fair. But what do Anglo geographers know? To the Navahos this is holy land, loaded with divine energy; they have never heard of "real estate." They fought the Utes, the Spanish and then the Anglos to hold on to it. In 1863-64, Kit Carson, who is the Eichmann of Navaho history (old men still spit at his name), came through with the U.S. Army, slaugh-tered the tribe's flocks, burned their corn fields and peach or-

* The Navaho language is part of the Athabascan language family. Other Athabascan peoples include the Apache as well as the Dogribs, Carriers, Na-Denes, Yellowknives and other tribes of the Canadian Arctic and Alaska. The Navahos themselves came down from the north into the Southwestern desert only three or four centuries ago.

chards and marched them into exile at Bosque Redondo on the harsh prairies of eastern New Mexico. Of the 8,000 Navahos sent on the Long Walk, as it was called, a third perished of hunger, exposure, disease and outright murder; many others were sold into slavery.

When the Treaty of 1868 was signed, allowing the surviving remnants of the Dineh to return home, Barboncito, one of the headmen, said, "After we get back to our country, it will brighten up again and the Navahos will be as happy as the land, black clouds will rise and there will be plenty of rain. Corn will grow in abundance and everything will look happy." The Navahos see their country through the eyes of lovers; their songs reiterate its beauty, refract it, enunciate it, over and over. Those furrowed, dull hills, like knees and laps draped with rose-colored silk in the light of dusk; that distant mountain, jade in a flint shroud of unfallen rain; green corn against roan cliff: all these are beautiful; beautiful and therefore holy, an equation Anglos have missed. The Navaho word for god is *Yei,* or "beautiful one."

One summer day in Window Rock, the tribal capital, I peered over a floor covered with aerial photographs of the eastern border of the reservation, from Window Rock north to Shiprock. It reminded me of nothing so much as a flight I once took from New Delhi to Teheran over the high, rugged plateau of Central Asia. There were the same naked mountains, the hogback ridges and cuestas; the same tenuous scrub forests surviving in what little rain shadow the mountains provided. Arroyos feathered down into the valleys, joining together to form rivers that were more mud and sand than water.

Life in such a land requires patience, cunning and nerve. Looking at the photographs of the Navaho country, I could see where, in the crook of a wash, an Indian had built a dam out of alluvial stones to hold and trap the occasional water that ran down out of the Chuskai Mountains. There was a fenced rectangle of corn and a tiny peach orchard, the usual crude brush sheep corral, the same kind desert people build all across the earth from Jordan to Tibet to Dinetah. A cluster of hogans, representing several families, cottonwoods and a skein of pickup tire tracks leading off toward the highway and the trading post. Mutton, wool, blankets, turquoise and silver, traded for trucks, gas, coffee, guns and, of course, sugar and salt, the magic white powders of the white man; and the "water that banishes reason," alcohol—cheap red wine, brandy, whiskey that goes down your throat like napalm, burning your spirit away.

It is a delicate way of life; it all leads back, ultimately, to that intermittent thread of water that sometimes, sometimes, doesn't trickle down out of the mountains. If the rains and snows fail, the corn and sage and peach trees and piñon will perish, the sheep and goats and cattle and horses will die; and the people, too, if they do not move. It has happened down here before. Chaco Canyon, Mesa Verde, Betatakin and Keet Seel, the pueblos of the San Juan, all were abandoned because of drought; sinister lacunae, those empty rooms and fields gone to brush and thorn. All history down here is merely a thin skin on the surface of hydrology, a pluvial accident.

One summer up on the northern part of the reservation I drove down from Shonto to the Black Mesa Trading Post to buy groceries and pick up my mail. A very drunk Navaho cowboy came in, bent and bowlegged: a twisty little man doused with dust, Stetson pushed back, boot heels run down. He came up to me, breathing wine like a dragon, and took my arm. "Hey, man," he said, leaning his face close, "I heard old Elvis died. I was sure sorry to hear that." I didn't know what to say; it was as if he thought Elvis and I were clan brothers, friends or something. "Yeah, it was too bad," I said finally. "I guess his heart gave out or something." "Yeah," said the Navaho cowboy as if he hadn't heard me, "Elvis died. Elvis and Hitler, two of your greatest leaders, dead." He shook his head in commiseration and stumbled away down the aisle of saddles and ropes and hats.

One collects incidents like this on the reservation, hoping to put together some kind of mosaic that makes sense—or, rather, *Anglo* sense; but all one ends up with is a bigger, better cryptogram. Was the Navaho cowboy completely ignorant of Anglo ways and boozily misconnecting two Anglo names he had happened to remember? Or was he (as I suspect) subtly joking me about the quality of Anglo heroes? Navahos have an acute sense of humor, especially when it comes to *belagonas,* as they call us Anglos.

I dated a Navaho girl for a time; her name was Barbara Salt, and she had been brought up off the reservation, in Los Angeles, where her father worked in a defense plant. She was too, too beautiful. When she combed her shining black hair or spent hours piecing together beadwork on a tiny loom (barbaric colors: it looked as if she were weaving a new coat for a Gila monster), she looked so out-of-time, it stole your heart away. Yet her talk was half filled with surfboards and flying saucers and smoking dope in convertibles speeding down Mulholland Drive, and half with remembered childhood stories of life back on the reservation and visits to her relatives, who lived north of Kayenta. Her grandparents still ran sheep up there, though they were both nearly blind and could barely hobble after their flocks on brittle legs. Like many radical young Indians, Barbara refused to admit that her people had come across into the Americas from Asia. "We were always here," she said. "We always lived right where we live now, between the four sacred mountains."

Anthropologists, with their blood-type maps and archeological burrowings and trait lists, have pretty well established that the first Americans came across Beringia tens of thousands of years ago, and that the Navahos drifted down from the Arctic only three or four hundred years ago—these American Bedouin are, remarkably, transplanted tundra-dwellers. But when I tried to tell Barbara that, she would have none of it. "Look, I don't know how we got here—maybe we evolved here, maybe we came out of a spaceship—but I know one thing, I ain't no damn Chinese!" Actually, Navaho origin myth says that the People emerged from an ice cave, a bleak, wintry womb in the side of a mountain in southwestern Colorado. Old-time Navahos still make pilgrimages to this birthing place of their tribe. Perhaps, in one way or another, all of these stories are equally true—all dreams, all songs.

Sometimes I think everything is crazy down there; or, rather, that *we* are so crazy we will never comprehend it: *Dineh* are *Dineh, belagona* are *belagona,* and never the twain shall meet.

One spring afternoon I rode north out of Flagstaff with an old Navaho in a brand-new supercharged pickup truck. He wore a purple-satin cowboy shirt with white piping, Tony Lama boots, doubleknit Western slacks, a heavy beaver-felt twenty-gallon hat, a string tie with a silver thunderbird at his throat and a digital timepiece with a fire-coral—studded band. There was an eagle plume hanging from the rear-view mirror. He was a fine-looking man, a person of substance. "I'm goin' as far as Tuba City," he said.

We accelerated out of Flagstaff, faster and faster, settling down to a rock-steady hundred miles an hour up that bumpy road that curved northeast into the Navaho Nation. The tape player blasted out an Indian chant. There was a lot of traffic on the road, but the old man never slowed down.

"I'm gonna drive you home in my '52 pickup truck. Hey ya ya ya, hey ya ya ya," the cassette player chanted: one of those modern Indian songs, called "Forty-niners."

We passed Magic Mountain and then Gray Mountain, that honky-tonk reservation border town with its string of hitchhiking drunks, and crossed the corroded red desert that descends to the Little Colorado River. The old man pulled a Cobra CB microphone from under the dash and talked away to somebody in the intricate, slurred Navaho tongue—wool and mutton futures? An epidemic of *chinde,* or ghosts, out by Chilchinbito? On we went, at one hundred miles per hour, steady and sure as fate.

Finally, close to Tuba City, we hit a jammed herd of tourist traffic snailing up a long, winding hill behind a Winnebago.

There were a lot of cars ahead of us—a dozen, maybe—and a blind curve ahead. The old man pulled out around them without a pause and floored it.

We were about two thirds of the way past the pack when another Indian in a pickup truck, also speeding, rounded the curve above us. He leaned on his horn; the old grandfather leaned on *his*. Neither touched the brake. We headed toward each other like a couple of jousting bighorns.

There was no way we could get by. There was the Winnebago on our right, blocking the right lane, and an arroyo to the left, dropping off steeply, going over which would have been like steering straight into the grave. But the old wizard, deadpan, kept the pedal to the floor, as if there was nobody else on the road. I instinctively cringed and punched my foot down on an imaginary brake pedal.

At the last instant, the old man simply pulled over into the right-hand lane, veering into the Winnebago broadside, driving it off the road, over the shoulder and into the desert. I looked back to see the colossal recreational vehicle, big as five hogans and costing more than the annual income of ten Navaho sheepherding families, bouncing away across the dunes, tearing through a barbed-wire fence.

We were still doing a hundred. When I looked over at the old Navaho, he was grinning at me out of the corner of his face; and then he began to laugh, "'Eh 'eh 'eh," and suddenly we were both laughing together at the mad perfection of it all.

Strange things happen down on the Navaho Nation, things that seem to have leaked out of a dream into the real, solid world. Witches, for instance: Navahos believe that some people who lead everyday, normal lives on the surface are in reality *brujos,* black magicians. Navaho witches are a particularly bad lot: they eat human flesh and dig up corpses to make a dust called corpse powder, which they squirt on their sleeping victims to kill them—a kind of infectious death. You never know who might be a witch: you might see a coyote sneaking around your sheep pen at night and take a shot at it with your varmint rifle and the next morning find your brother or mother or cousin lying there dead, with your bullet in them. Suspected witches are still occasionally executed in the back country of the reservation.

Reality is, when you get right down to it, consensual: a tribe or a society makes up its mind what it is going to see and then it sees it; delusion by plurality. What the Navahos see and feel is no truer, no falser than our own sensory world; but it certainly has more magic than ours. And I like that. We have exorcised our world too well: "Before Christianity, all power came from magic," Lawrence Durrell wrote. "After it, from money." All too true.

There is magic going on down in the Nation, but it is illusive. The great rituals of the tribe, the Sings or Ways, are not given at set places and times. They are performed when a family or a clan wants to accomplish something, often a curing or healing: they are usually given far from towns and highways, and whites are not welcome. In fact, Navahos from other clans are not welcome. When Peter MacDonald, tribal chairman (known to some young Navahos as "the Navaho Nixon"), showed up at a ceremony near Teec Nos Pos, his bodyguards were beaten and his limousine trashed, and he had to flee in a tribal police car.

Ghost stories are a kind of spiritual pornography, but I have one that is too good not to tell. An anthopologist friend and his wife, who worked on the same anomalous research project that employed me, were driving across the reservation one night on one of the back roads. It was way past midnight, they saw nothing except an occasional goat, a gaunt feral steer, a half-wild horse . . .

Suddenly, out of nowhere, an ancient Navaho woman appeared in their headlights, hobbling along in the same direction they were going, alone. They pulled up next to her and my friend's wife rolled down the window. "Would you like a ride?" she asked, looking into the oldest face in North America, wrinkled and seamed like an ancient tortoise's. But instead of answering, the crone began to screech at them, shaking her fists in the air. They drove away, and when they looked back, the old woman had vanished and a big, pale dog was running down the road after them.

They told a Navaho friend about it later, and he said, "Witch." "What would you have done?" they asked him. "Shoot her or run over her with the truck. Or just get the hell out of there."

I know a couple of other stories just as unbelievable, but I think I'll save them; stories, like certain cheeses, improve with age.

There are tales you hear down on the reservation of stranger, more powerful medicine men: not Singers, the men who give the great rituals, or herb doctors or witches, but *magi,* something like the siddhis of the East. There is one, for instance, who is supposed to be several hundred years old and lives in a cave with two mountain lions up a nameless canyon somewhere. I believe these stories somehow: they remind me irresistibly of tales of such Asian saints as Milarepa, Han Shan, Lao-Tse and Bodhidharma. And there is no reason why such sumptuous mysteries should reveal themselves to white Americans, spiritual paupers that we are. Native America has always guarded its secrets jealously. Who built Tiahuanaco, that cryptic Andean city on the Altiplano? The Saint Louis Snake Mound? There are no photographs of Crazy Horse; both he and Wovoka, prophet of the ghost dance, are buried in unknown graves, one near Pyramid Lake, the other on the Powder River, somewhere on the lost continent of America.

Nowhere in this continent are people and land so inextricably bound together as in Dinetah. Navaho place-names celebrate the actualities of survival—the Zen of earth, if you will. Corn-fields. Many Farms. The Chuskai ("White Fir Trees") Mountains. Dinnehotso, "The Edge of the Meadow." Bad Water, Sweetwater, Mexican Water, Bitter Water; Chilchinbite ("Water in the Sumacs"), Oljeto ("Moonlit Water"), Shato

("Sunshine Water Springs"). Black Rock, Rough Rock, Round Rock, Window Rock, Spider Rock, Red Rock, Owl Rock, Kicking Rock, Baby Rocks; Two Gray Hills, Hummingbird, Burnt Corn, Greasewood . . . Each name is a piece of primitive *musique concrète*; and each name is also the germ of a story, the thread around which a yarn is spun . . .

Kicking Rock, for instance, along the San Juan: They say old Kicking Rock sat by a narrow place in the trail high above the river, and when travelers passed by, he would say, "Um, my knee is feelin' kind of stiff. I'd better stretch it." And then he would kick the travelers into the river below, where his monstrous children fed on their bodies. One day the Hero Twins came along—monster-slayers; they cut Kicking Rock into pieces with their potent obsidian daggers and threw the pieces into the river. Kicking Rock's children devoured their father, exclaiming how delicious the meat was: "Father killed us a *good* traveler this time!" Typical Navaho humor.

Some of the other place-names tell a different kind of story: Laguna Canyon and Marsh Pass, for instance, between Kayenta and Cow Springs, north of Black Mesa. Within living memory (two generations perhaps), these were rich sloughs, oases. There are tales of great migratory flocks of geese and ducks gathering there, and deer, elk, beaver. But about a century ago, as the Navahos became successful herders, their sheep and goats multiplied far beyond the carrying capacity of the land; they literally devoured these microenvironments by "strip grazing"—the pastoral equivalent of strip mining. The range was gnawed to the roots, the soil was sucked away by the wind, the waters ran off through a maze of arroyos. Wasteland with green, ironic names: a Marsh Pass dry as a mummy, a Laguna Canyon with lakes of sand.

But however poor the earth is, down here it is loved. Earth, land, is the ultimate Navaho reality. There is nothing greater. Navaho political power does not grow out of the barrel of a gun: it grows out of the land, like corn, like sagebrush, like the dream flowers of jimson weed. Gods sprout like dry weeds from exhausted soil.

In the remotest northern part of the Navaho Nation, just to the south of the San Juan River, north of No Man's and Skeleton mesas, is the mountain called Navaho. It is as remote as a place can be these days: it is a long, long way from anywhere to this jade-and-cobalt peak that rises like an apparition from the rose-colored desert.

Navaho Mountain—they also call it Pollen, or War, or War God Mountain—is the grandest thing in the landscape. It draws the eye for hundreds of miles, from Page, Arizona, to Cedar Mesa, Utah. In the summer it pulls rain from the dry sky: you see a great hump of nickel cumulus, a gray plume of rain and the black mass of the mountain itself. If you took peyotl, closed your eyes and thought "Mountain," this is the mountain you would see: Navaho. From the first time I sighted it peering at me over the edge of the world as I drove west from Black Mesa Trading Post toward Cow Springs, I wanted to go there. It seemed the essence of everything reticent, unknowable, in the country of the Navaho.

It took me almost a year to get there; and by that time I had picked up a whole bagful of stories about the place. An old anthropologist I met in Gallup who was studying Navaho alcoholism by drinking himself into stupefaction at the Club Mexico and the All-American every night told me of an odd Navaho clan who lived north of the mountain. When the Dineh were deported to Bosque Redondo in 1863, a few of the northernmost Navahos escaped to the furrowed, confused country between the San Juan River and Navaho Mountain. They intermarried with a renegade band of Piutes who lived in the area, and avoided all contact with Anglos for a long, long time. Their descendants still live up there around the mountain, a kind of lost tribe: tall, diffident, backward people. Many of them still shun pickup trucks in favor of horses—and pickup trucks are as Navaho as turquoise or sheep. (What horses were to the nineteenth-century Plains tribes, pickups are to Navahos—objects so perfect that they are endowed with *mana*,

bulging beyond their physical boundaries. One tribal government pamphlet, out of Canoncito, New Mexico, begins a short
history of the Navaho with the classic line, "A long, long time
ago, there weren't any pickup trucks"—as if the first black
Model A pickup rattling onto the reservation back in the
twenties, full of Ute Peyote Church missionaries from Sleeping
Ute Mountain, were some kind of primal alpha. Someone
should trace the spread of pickup trucks through the Navaho
Nation: it would make a fascinating history.) At Navaho
Mountain, the old anthropologist said, truck time had not yet
begun.

The old anthropologist reminded me of some old, fuddled
Colonel Blimp in India in the heyday of the raj: dry, caustic,
foolish, with a colossal red nose and steel-gray hair that looked
as if it was cut with a bad knife. Decades ago he had done one
of the first Indian drinking studies, in the rough-and-tumble
bars of Los Angeles and Reno. He told a hundred tales of
endless nights bar-hopping in jalopies with the last Kickapoos,
a hundred hilarious disasters. Now he and his thin, sarcastic
wife were living in a fine adobe on the highest hill in Gallup;
she collected Navaho blankets, while he poured the whiskey
down far into the night, in the name of Science.

Other stories about the mountain told of eagles, turquoise,
witches on the roads and lions in the trees. The funny thing
was, no one I talked to had actually been there: all the stories I
heard were well-used, rubbed blurry and vague with age. This
lent them, and the mountain itself, an even deeper aura of
mystery.

Almost a year after my first summer on the reservation, Barbara Salt and I drove down from Colorado to walk around the
western edge of the mountain to Rainbow Bridge. A friend had
a friend who had hiked there years ago, and we had a set of
directions: "Drive north from Shonto (road bad); at Utah state
line, road forks—take left-hand fork (road worse); drive ap-
prox. ten miles, to ruins of old Rainbow Lake (stone walls,

hard to find); look for north by northwest, possibly marked, possibly not (WATCH TRAIL CAREFULLY—easy to wander off on herding trails and waste half a day); first reliable water is at Eight-Mile Camp, a spring in the cliff on the right-hand side; the trail the rest of the way is easy to follow, if you don't miss the turn to Redbud Pass."

Ironically, Barbara didn't know much more about the geography of the Navaho country than I did. It was her lost homeland, her Palestine; but like anyone drifting home from Diaspora, she had more emotions about her homeland than facts. After all, she spoke only a few phrases of Navaho, while most reservation Navahos, even the young, are unfluent in English; and Barbara was a real city girl, pure Los Angeles, while Navaho reservation life is old-timey, cowboy, like nothing else in America, really.

As we crossed that strip of sleazy borderland around Farmington, she went through something like culture shock. Shops full of junk, mean-faced police, the alky squalor of the Turquoise and Zia bars: it looked like something out of Tijuana or Landi Kotal on the Khyber Pass, the same poverty, vice and bald avarice, the evil electricity generated wherever the First World rubs up too hard against the Third. "What is this place, anyway?" she muttered.

"Ugliness on the way to the magic mountain."

We passed the Four Corners Power Plant, the tall stacks trickling across the sky a subtle pall of Navaho coal burning, the tall, high-tension lines leading toward LA. It was a hot, bright day; the hills glinted like heaps of broken glass. We passed through Shiprock, that classic Navaho town; people were selling melons, corn, tamales and fry bread by the intersection, where one highway ran south ninety-nine miles to Gallup and the other road led west to Biklabito, Rattlesnake, Kayenta, Tuba City. We turned west there for Navaho Mountain.

From Shiprock to Black Mesa Trading Post, where you turn north for Navaho Mountain, is an airy journey; the land is so immense that you feel as if you are levitating, swooping and soaring across the desert fifty, a hundred feet up. That road turns people into hawks. The wind howls across the bronze land, with scattered humps of hogans here and there and the delicate litter of pastoral camps, sheep pens, corrals, a tin trailer . . . A herd of pied horses trembles in the uncertain sun.

We camped that night up near the ruined Anasazi city of Beta-takin. It took us half of the next day to drive to the base of Navaho Mountain. The road, through Shonto and Inscription House, past a lone ugly mission, was terrible: bedrock, wind-drifted sand, big loose stones. We had worried about a spring blizzard catching us, but the weather, as usual, had doubled back on itself: the sky was cloudless, and desperately hot.

Just past the Utah state line the road forked, right to Navaho Mountain Trading Post, left to nowhere. We turned left across a flat stony desert broken by ravines, studded with brush. A field of dead corn, a collapsed fence of sticks. When this road ran out, we started walking. The upper slopes of Navaho Mountain, still white with snow, loomed over us to the south-east. But down where we were, down in the rocks, it was like a blast furnace.

We crossed Chaiyahi Flats and a series of deep canyons: First Canyon, Horse Canyon, Dome. I had expected to find water, lots of it, in the canyon bottoms, but there was none, not a drop. Lizards watched us from the rocks with cold, uncaring eyes. A buzzard hovered in the sky, motionless, as if hung on a hook. We hiked a trail of broken rocks that cut our feet and blazed as if they had spilled out of a forge.

As the afternoon wore on, the land fell away to the north and west, toward Lake Powell. We looked down into the earth, into enormous basements of bedrock. Here were cruel iron buttes, moon-colored domes, mosques of melting butter, rocks pulled and twisted like putty and shot full of holes, seraglios and languorous blond stone.

We crossed Sunset Pass (Yabuts Pass is the Piute name for it) toward evening; the trail dropped off headlong into Cliff

Canyon. We picked our way down the crumbling trail. It was slow going. Dark fell just as we came out onto the narrow canyon floor; we stumbled on down to Eight-Mile Camp by dim flashlight. I found the spring, dribbling corrosive green from a crack in the cliff, and filled our empty canteens; we hadn't seen a drop of water all day till then. Barbara built a fire of cottonwood sticks, dry, frost pale, that burned quickly. We boiled up tea and dried stew. A gritty wind rattled the trees, sobbed in the cliffs. The canyon was narrow there, and across the narrow seam of sky, dark tufts of cloud scudded south.

"Is there a storm coming in?"

"Maybe. This weather is real neurotic. Can't tell what it's going to do."

"Well, I wish it would do something," she said. "I'd just as soon hike through snow; at least you can melt it and drink it. Is it always this dry?"

"We must just be in the wrong canyon. With all that snow up on the mountain, there must be melt water somewhere. It's strange there's none here."

"The mountain is keeping it all for himself."

We wouldn't see Navaho Mountain, the cold, dark mass of it, anymore. But actually we were inside one of the cracks in the great bulge of sandstone over magma that forms the peak; we were down in the hard hide of the mountain itself. We slept uneasily, disturbed by the wind, the squeaky plucked violins of the bats and thoughts that flashed like fire in the blackness. When we touched, the static jumped between our skins.

The next day we left most of our gear at camp and hiked on for Rainbow Bridge. The sky was powder blue and hot as a skillet. We saw only a few sheep tracks, probably strays, and the prints of a lone horse. Farther on, where the trail met a red stone cliff and turned east, was another spring and a row of Anasazi petroglyphs—big-headed gods, squiggling snakes, forked lightning—scratched there on the rock to guard the place. Next to the petroglyphs some Navaho had scrawled his own proprietary sign: INDIAN COUNTRY, it said. Below it was a rough drawing of an archetypal Navaho family, a man in a tall

Stetson, a woman in a long dress, a son and daughter, all holding hands in a row. "Here we are," the drawing seemed to say. "Now *we* live here: this land is ours."

"Only an Indian could live down here," Barbara said, sounding proud.

"Yeah. No one else is stubborn or simple enough."

She thought that over, decided it wasn't an insult, said "Yeah" and laughed. Anyhow, it was true. You would have to go to the back country of Central Asia or the Andean Plateau of South America to find people still living in such desiccated, marginal microenvironments, patching subsistence together out of scraps and leavings of runoff and alluvium. In the right hands, poverty can be a fine art: Indians are masters of it.

Later that morning we came to Redbud Pass. Wetherill and his party, the first whites to visit Rainbow Bridge, came through in 1909, led by the Piute guide Nasjah Begay (his name means "son of Mr. Spider"). They had to blast their way through Redbud Pass with dynamite to get their horses up and over. The defile is still narrow and steep; the trail winds its way through boulders and scrub juniper trees. As we descended into Bridge Canyon, we passed a barricade built out of brush and a falling-down gate of sticks and wire—a Navaho stock fence. On a boulder by the trail, someone had written: LOST A HORSE HERE. CLYDE WHISKERS. Whiskers is a not uncommon family name among Navahos. Like Redhouse, Tso ("Skinny") Begay ("Son of"), Greyeyes, Yellowhair, Starlight, Salt, Many-goats, Peaches, it was a name with a living, vivid nucleus. I liked "Clyde Whiskers." I wondered who he was, how he lived back here—sheepherding, of course—and whether he ever found his horse. A mile or so down Bridge Canyon, we came to a long pool of water under the overhanging rock; the reflected ripples licked like flames on the sandstone roof. The water was shockingly cold and clear as a lens; the dust boiled off of us like smoke when we bathed.

Just about everyone who knows anything about the American West has read about Rainbow Bridge and seen a photograph of it. It is one of those geological anomalies, like Half Dome or Old Faithful, that Americans seize on and sentimentalize, while they lay waste the rest of the wilderness. I suppose at one time, before Lake Powell was backed up to it, this soaring ribbon of sandstone three hundred-odd feet above Bridge Creek must have been a compelling place. Powerful. The Navahos once treated it as a shrine: they called it *nonnezoshi,* or "the rainbow of stone." Rainbows are one of the cornerstones of Navaho metaphysics, personified as the Rainbow People, guardians of the universe. (Tibetans have a similar belief.)

But with Lake Powell and its marinas, powerboats and vacationers only two miles down canyon (today the lake reaches all the way to the base of the rainbow), most of the magic was gone. Accessibility, ease, the great vices of America, had squeezed the juice out of the metaphor and turned the power off. The gods had left for wherever gods go.

When Barbara and I got there that afternoon, there was a mob of houseboaters from the lake gathered around the base of the bridge where the trail runs under the arch. They clicked away with their cameras and chattered like daws. A radio was playing, and its tinny music itched in our ears after the profound stillness of the canyons.

We didn't like running into the lake people: after all of our bloody hard traveling, it just didn't seem fair to find them there. And I doubt if they liked seeing us much, either: a dark, sumptuous girl who looked like she *lived* back in those terrible sandstone mazes, and some kind of back-country bohemian mountaineer, both of them with huge packs and cottonwood walking sticks.

"How'd you folks get here?" One pink old man asked us querulously; he wore a billed cap that said: ALL FISHERMEN ARE LIARS, INCLUDING ME. When we told him we had walked in from the far side of Navaho Mountain, two days, the lake people all shook their heads: "Should've taken the boat. It's easy as pie. In another couple of years the lake will be right here, and you won't have to walk at all then."

"Are you an Indian, honey?" a woman asked Barbara sweetly.

They weren't bad people, of course; you would have had to

be a real fundamentalist archdruid not to feel at least a sneaky liking for them: good old middle Americans, stolid, salty, with a dour brand of humor. But we really didn't want to see them or their lake *down there* in that country whose body is petrified sand, whose spirit is denial. Some places should be left alone; this was one of them.

After a few minutes Barbara and I went off a ways by ourselves, found a spot of shade below a rock, drank our water and shared a Mandarin orange. A half hour later we headed back toward Eight-Mile Camp and the silence and solitude of the canyons.

The rest of the trip was much more interesting. We found we had forgotten to pack one of the stuff sacks of food, and we ran completely out of provisions. Dinner that night was a lump of cheese and a chip of chocolate apiece, and that was it. The next day we had to hike out hungry. It was another cloudless, baleful day; the land seemed rinsed in fire. We left early, but the sun caught us on the climb up to Yabuts Pass. It was a 1,500-vertical-foot slog; perhaps 95 degrees and zero humidity. We drank our canteens dry halfway up, and then we were out of water.

The hike to the car was the worst walk I have ever done, six and a half miles that seemed endless. The quiet of the canyons was suddenly not peaceful at all, but oppressive, vaguely menacing. The cold white summit of Navaho Mountain looked disdainfully down on us, toiling through the chaos of stone. I poured out a spoonful of blood from my boots when we reached the car.

We didn't make it to the highway till after dark, and it was another hour east to Kayenta, where there was a café open. We bought Navaho tacos there and mutton stew and coffee. The food tasted better than any mystery. I didn't care if I never saw Navaho Mountain again; that short-order greasy spoon was shrine enough for me.

That night we drove back up to Colorado, staying awake on Methedrine tablets from the medical kit, bitter as gall; listening to Wolf Man Jack on the radio. A few weeks later Barbara

drove north for Alaska, to work on a salmon boat for the summer. I never heard a word from her again.

In time, of course, the miseries and disappointments of the trip
went away, and what I remembered probably never happened,
except in the imagination. I dreamed about that crazy journey
many times—it stuck deep in my psyche, down in the vague
part of the mind where memory recombines, fantastical, to
form dreams. Again and again, I walked those hard trails,
following Barbara around the edge of a shadow mountain, a
mountain of unknowing . . . It had become a kind of a fairy
tale.

Three years later I came back, again in the spring, to walk
all the way around the mountain. This year the desert was wet
with rain, the road up from Shonto ran red with earth, the
skies were cool and cloudy. The rain had wet the range till it
glowed. The top of Navaho Mountain was hidden in mists.

It was strange, and a shade melancholy, walking the trail to
Eight-Mile Camp alone. I thought of Barbara and wondered
where she was, whether she had ever come back here and
walked these lonely trails again. I even imagined, foolishly,
coming to Eight-Mile Camp in the evening and finding her
there, under the cottonwood trees, combing her long brooding
hair . . . But of course there was no one there; Eight-Mile
Camp was deserted.

The next day I hiked down to Rainbow Bridge and camped a
couple of miles up canyon from the bridge. And the day after
that I crossed the whole north side of the mountain.

This was the country I had dreamed was there, a tangled
web of cliffs, towers, mesas, ravines. It drizzled on and off that
morning. I crossed a stony mesa, a herd of sheep in the distance, but no people. Oak Canyon was a cleft of green, green
cottonwoods, like jade set in bone. Beyond was a maze of
canyons; looking at my USGS map only gave names to the
confusion. Nasjah (Navaho for spider) Canyon. Moepitz Canyon, a Piute name whose meaning I did not know. Lehi Can-

yon, a name dug up out of the Bible, probably Mormon in origin. Trail, Desha, Anasazi canyons. Cha Canyon: *cha* is Navaho for either beaver or excrement. (I favored the latter, as there was a huge rock of suggestive shape where the trail dipped into what should have been Cha Canyon.)

I kept thinking I would run into somebody. I passed more herds of sheep and goats, and messages written on the rock by the omnipresent Clyde Whiskers: "CLYDE WHISKERS & MARY MANYGOATS." "CLYDE WHISKERS '70. "CLYDE WHISKERS WAS HERE." Perhaps, I thought, Clyde Whiskers was a Navaho Everyman, a Native American Kilroy; perhaps, like them, he was always there, but he had never been there at all: like Coyotl, or Avalokitesvara.

It was a day of omens and portents. About midday I found an abandoned hogan in a draw full of cottonwoods. There was still a metal cot inside and a little iron stove with a frying pan and a coffeepot on top; but the cobwebs in the door hung in thick shrouds, and one of the dried-mud walls was falling in. No one had been there for a long, long time. The canyon was full of a loud, buzzing silence. Death, I thought. Among the traditional Navahos, when somebody dies in a hogan, everybody moves away, for death is unclean, *wrong,* a kind of contagious darkness. That must have happened here; and now the place belonged only to the *chinde,* those who have left the bright world of the living behind and who have no love for the living.

I thought for a moment of taking the coffeepot, tying it on my pack—it was a good old enameled one, blue, with white flecks like snow—but then I thought, No, I don't want to drink coffee with the dead, and so I left it and walked on.

It was one of those days in which everything is supernaturally charged with a meaning almost readable, but cryptic; the world strains with revelation. To the south the whole northern face of Navaho Mountain—cliffs, gorges, steep forests—took up the horizon; to the north the country grew more and more intricate, tessellations of ruby, rust and chalk under haze; above, a skyful of clouds pulled east in the wind. I walked east with it, crossing mesa after mesa, canyon after canyon. I saw more herds of sheep and goats in the distance, grazing on the stony brush; a clump of beehive-shaped hogans with smoke spiraling up, and a dog barking; a log sheep pen against a far canyon wall; but no people, no one at all . . . Only sitting beneath a Douglas fir in midafternoon, something moved out of the corner of my eye, and I looked up to see a mountain lion, like a long, golden shadow, flow up over the rimrock and vanish. Like a shooting star, it all happened in an instant. A beautiful disturbance rippled slowly across my eye and mind.

Toward the end of the day, a horseman rode out of the southeast. He came riding up to me, a rawboned old man on a big gaunt horse, riding slow, with a sack slung over his saddlehorn. He was long and narrow, with a long, curious face. He grinned and raised a huge hand in greeting as he reined in his horse. *"Yaatahey,"* he said.

"Yaatahey. How far is it to the trading post?"

He cocked his head and laughed. *"St'o',"* he said, pointing south over the edge of the mountain. He pointed to the sack: *"Co'n,"* Then he gestured at me with his great hand: *"Ca'fon'ya'?*

"California?" He nodded. "No, Colorado."

"Co'lo'a'do. Ah." He pointed to himself: *"Oo'tah."*

He sat up there on his horse, that giant, ancient man—he almost creaked in the wind—smiling down at me, studying me, a *belagona* walking around the sacred mountain alone with a crazy orange thing strapped to his back like a hump. It would make a good story to tell his friends later: "I met this crazy *belagona* crossing Desha Canyon . . . mebbe he was a lost missionary . . . mebbe he was looking for gold . . . "

He raised his hand again, as if in benediction, spurred his horse gently into motion and headed on down the trail. I looked back once; he was turned in the saddle, watching me. I waved; he turned away. I started on my way again, heading for the wrong side of the mountain, while the old man rode home into the time of stone.

I crossed No Man's Mesa just as dusk fell; the trail became a rough road, and there were more hogans off toward Navaho Begay, "Son of Navaho," the small peak on the eastern shoulder of the big mountain. The desert was radiant. To the northeast the goblin country of the San Juan submerged in a slumberous glow. I was dog-tired. Twenty-two miles today, according to the map.

As darkness fell, a pickup truck came speeding out of No Man's Mesa: a young Navaho man, two sleek young women and two children. The women wore heavy silver, velvet in slurried colors of maroon and green. "Going to the trading post?" one asked in soft, broken English. "You can have a ride."

I rode in the back; the stars came out; it got cold. We came to the trading post about eight o'clock, and I slept that night out back in the tall grass under the dark, hunched shoulder of the mountain.

I read somewhere that one of the highest peaks in North America once stood in the center of what is now Lake Superior. The story sounds too good to be true, but I pass it on to you for what it's worth. The mountain, the story goes, vanished millenniums ago, ground down by ice, wind, time. There is nothing left to show where it stood—only the invisible whorls in the magnetic skin of the earth, deep in the bedrock beneath the deep black waters of the lake. But the migrating geese that cross the lake still turn, they say, to avoid the vanished mountain. It still exists in their piano rolls of memory, rolled tight in those airy skulls.

Navaho Mountain is like that. There is the mountain of stone and soil, covered with timber; and there is the thick electric sediment of memories and dreams, arched in a mountain more perfect than anything on earth.

I went to Navaho Mountain one last time, determined to climb to the summit. There, I thought, I would find some kind of transcendent sign, some kind of answer (though I wasn't even sure what the question was). If the sides of the mountain were so powerful, would not the summit be a capstone of pure mystery? So ran my thoughts, full of half-digested Jodorowsky and René Daumal.

I drove north from Tucson, where I had been staying with friends, up the long road through Phoenix, Flagstaff, Tuba City. Northeast of Tuba City there was snow on the ground; the sky was black and windy. It was November and the mountain would be cold, but I kept going.

The dirt roads north of Shonto were deep in red muck and molten snow, hard going. I bought cady bars, canned beef stew and cheese at Navaho Mountain Trading Post, and asked the trader about the route to the top. "No problem," he said. "Blind man couldn't miss it. Construction crew's been workin' on the road up there for weeks. If you had a four-wheel drive, you could drive all the way to the top."

This wasn't at all what I had expected, but it was too late to turn back now. I followed his directions, and as the sun set I was crawling my way up the rutted mud and stone of the mesa. Finally I came to a collection of heavy equipment, pickup trucks, Cats and Thiokol tractors, parked in a circle of gouged earth. The road went up steeply from there. It was already getting cold and there was nobody around, so I decided to camp. I unfolded the back seat of the station wagon, spread out my sleeping bag, ate the beef stew cold out of the can and fell asleep.

Sometime later I awoke to the sound of a diesel grumbling around about fifty feet from my car. I looked out and there were four or five men in hard hats trying to load a small diesel tractor up onto a trailer in the dark. "Just a cunt hair to the left, Joe!" one of them shouted. "Well, *you* try it then, smartass!" "Shut up and back it in again." "*Haw haw haw!* If ya can't aim any better'n that, I don't see how ya ever get a piece a ass." Night on the sacred mountain. I felt like the king of fools.

The next morning there was no one around, and I put on my

pack and began to trudge up the mountain. The road ran between steep forests and sandstone cliffs, following a power
line. The snow got deeper the higher I climbed, and it was hard
going. Off to the south, a storm was brewing: darkness over
Black Mesa, the horizon gone in red-tinged clouds, like glowing heaps of slag. The treetops shook in the wind.

The road gave out, or I lost it. I began to slog straight up the
mountainside, breaking through snow up to my waist. I was
near the top now, and suddenly it seemed worthwhile: the
whole long drive up the length of Arizona and the hike up
through the frozen mud and the wet snow.

I looked up, and a face was looking down at me, silhouetted
against the sky. Round, brown and smiling, it wore a plastic
hard hat with the words NAVAHO POWER AUTHORITY printed
across it. "Hey, what you doin' up here?" the Navaho asked.

I didn't know what to say. "Oh, just looking around. How
about you?"

A couple of other Navahos appeared. "We're working on the
power line up here. The line got blown down in a windstorm,
and we're puttin' it back up again. Navaho Power Authority
and Arizona Public Service."

"I heard there were mountain lions up here," I said, grasping
at a last wild straw.

They looked at each other: "Nope, never heard of any. No
mountain lion up here. I live here fifty years, I never heard of
one. But," he added brightly, obviously trying to help this
deranged *belagona,* "two weeks ago, I seen the biggest jackrabbit *you ever saw,* not two miles west of here. He must a been
two feet long!"

The wind roared, cold and blue, over the summit of Pollen
Mountain. They offered me a ride back down the mountain in
their Thiokol, and I accepted. I figured that they were *kind of*
medicine men—they were the only ones up there, anyway—and
that was good enough for me. On the way down they told me a
joke about a Hopi who went to a whorehouse, but I forget it.

The Delta

SOUTH OF THE SAN JUAN AND ITS CANYONS, BEYOND NAVAHO Mountain and Zuñi, the Colorado River unfolds, on and on, like a Chinese landscape scroll—rivers and mountains, pocket deserts and tiny turquoise seas, playas, cuestas, basins—unraveling to the very faded golden edges of the void . . .

If you followed the Colorado River far enough south—down through the Mogollon Rim country, past the Little Colorado, the Salt and the Gila, across the Sonoran Desert with its boneyard mountains and surreal giant-cactus forests—if you traveled to the very end, you would come to the Colorado Delta between Baja California, Sonora and the Sea of Cortez. After so many years, thousands of miles, of wandering the Colorado River country, it was no wonder that one day I found myself dreaming of the river's end. I saw it in my mind's eye: blue lagoons, golden sands and the heavy water, the iron-red blood of the West, rolling at last into the sea. I had to go there someday.

Looking through books and obscure maps, I found that the delta of the Colorado lies at latitude 31°53´, longitude 115°. It is an intricate place: choked on its own debris, the river fractures into long shards of laguna, sloughs and oxbows. Before the dams upriver cut off the flow of the Colorado and its tributaries, the delta was really wild, a dangerous place. In the spring, when the entire Colorado Basin emptied its dead snows and spring rains down that single slender channel, the delta was a raging, placeless place, neither earth nor sea. Whole islands drowned in a flood tide thick as library paste; sand spits were whipped away like paper cutouts; whole ranges of hills vanished. The map of the delta was one great blurry question mark: genesis, nameless.

In 1540, Hernando de Alarcón sailed up the Sea of Cortez and "discovered" the delta. The Cocopah Indians had lived there for centuries, and the Sand Papagos (more on them later) knew the place, but Indians never *discover* anything; they are just there, it seems, like the rocks, the ground water, the wild grass. Exploration of the delta went slowly. James Ohio Pattie, the intrepid trapper who had explored the depths of Glen Canyon in search of beaver, tried to cross the delta east to west in the 1820s, searching for a new route to California. He perished somewhere out there in the maze of creeks and marshes and salt dunes.

In 1857–58, Derby and Ives, two American naval officers, navigated the river all the way from the Sea of Cortez north to Callville, near the present location of Hoover Dam. For a time there was regular steamship service between Yuma and Callville and also in the delta itself: a Compania de Navigacion del Golfo de California S.A. operated between El Mayor and Santa Rosalie.

In 1922, Aldo Leopold, the American naturalist and writer, canoed the delta all the way from the American side of the border to the sea. He wrote of coyotes and bobcats prowling the riverbanks, and huge flocks of sandhill cranes falling like snow through the crisp indigo sky. Quail, deer, coons of thickets of mesquite and tornillo; everywhere the unseen presence of *el tigre*, the jaguar. It was like being back in the Pleistocene, Leopold wrote: "A hundred miles of lovely desolation, a vast flat bowl of wilderness rimmed by jagged peaks." It was a dangerous place, too. Leopold missed the forty-feet high tidal bore that rolled up through the delta on a full-moon night that same year, wrecking the Mexican ship *Topolobampo* and drowning a hundred souls.

All of that happened before the dams. The Colorado River has an average flow of 13 to 17 million acre-feet a year. (An acre-foot is the amount of water it takes to cover an acre to the depth of a foot.) Today, only 1.5 million acre-feet make it as far as Mexico; the rest is siphoned off in the United States by an elaborate system of tunnels, dams and canals to water Los Angeles, the Imperial Valley, Denver, the desert cities of Arizona, etc., etc. The last 1.5 million acre-feet are used by Mexico to irrigate farmlands north of the delta, through a six-hundred-mile-long network of canals. The Colorado River no longer reaches the sea; it is no longer a river, and its delta is a dead carcass, inhabited by a restless, bitter ghost. Still, I wanted to see the place, if only to exhume its remains, pay my respects. The maps of the delta I had showed such riddles as "Laguna Salada," "Volcano Lake," "Boat Slough"; phantom pieces of river such as the Paredones, the Abejos, the Nuevo, the Pescadero. There was a desert, el Desierto de los Chinos, where a party of Chinese immigrants had died of thirst. There would still be pockets of wildness here and there, I thought, and the ghosts of birds: silent song plumaged in a dry blue epidermis of air.

During World War II, the U.S. Army, fearing that the Germans would use Mexico as a base for invading the American South-west (which we stole from Mexico in the first place), somehow got the Mexican government to survey and draw up modern contour maps, suitable for military use. At least, that's the story I heard. Unfortunately, the project ran out of steam by the time the mapmakers were about a third of the way through the country, working north to south. There *were* maps of northern Mexico then, including the Colorado delta—but, of course, they were impossible to find. Finally I located a map store in Tucson, an appropriately strange little store that carried the maps. There was a master map on the wall; you picked out the maps you wanted from it, a clerk behind the counter called down to the basement, and a few minutes later a dumbwaiter ascended with your maps neatly rolled up inside.

With maps in hand, all I needed was a boat, a boat that could fit on or in my small car. I looked around and came up with a small inflatable boat of rubberized canvas, made in Europe. It rolled up into a canvas bag when deflated, and even the plastic oars collapsed like telescopes. You blew it up with a little foot pump. It was a quixotic craft, and I named it *Insh'Allah,* because when you got in it you were definitely entrusting yourself to God's mercy.

I left for the delta at dusk, in the middle of one of the worst winter storms in a decade. Snow was falling all the way from the Sierra Nevada to Ohio, and more sea storms were rolling in off the Pacific, crossing the northern California coast and becoming squall lines of snow when they reached the Sierra. The heater wasn't working in my car, and I had to drive wrapped in a sleeping bag and an old Army blanket, down mitts on my hands, a wool cap pulled down tight over my head: I looked like some kind of Andean spaceman. My breath fogged the windshield, and every few minutes I had to scrape the thin onionskin layers of ice off with my knuckles.

Sunset on Lizard Head Pass: in a break in the storm, the peaks glowed nacreous in the bleak red light. Around Dolores it began to rain. I crossed the San Juan River. South of Shiprock it began to snow again, big flakes spiraling toward me like a billion soft, slow bullets, straining my eyes to focus through them on the dim highway.

Chili and fry bread in a Gallup café. Zuñi Pueblo in the night, the sweet gray smell of piñon and cedar smoke in the air; no lights, a lone dog barking . . . At four in the morning I was crossing the high pine forests of the Fort and White River Apaches. Down through the Salt River Gorge. And then, as the first dawn light glowed on the eastern horizon, I saw the sprawling lights of Tucson ahead.

South. When you get to Tucson, you are south. I rolled down the car window, and already, at six-thirty on a winter morning, the air was lukewarm. Tucson is like a big chunk of Los Angeles dragged off into the Sonoran Desert and left there. The kids look like surfers with their blown-back white hair and Hawaiian shirts. Everybody has an ornate important car: a '46 Hudson painted electric blue, with three exhaust pipes; a silver pickup truck that sits eight feet high on oversized tires. I ordered breakfast in a drive-in restaurant where everything was square: square toast, square sausage and a square block of scrambled eggs that tasted like they had nothing to do with chickens.

I had crossed the heartland of the Colorado that night; I was in the lower Colorado Basin now, a country more akin to Mexico, southern California, than the high country of Colorado, Utah and the Navaho Nation.

The next day I drove west out of Tucson, across the Papago Indian Reservation. It drizzled at dawn, big drops of water sputtering in the dust, sending up an odor harshly sweet, as if a billion lighted matches were raining onto a field of dry incense. The damp earth shone like brown nylon.

Centuries ago—almost a thousand years, to be exact—the Papagos were one of the most highly civilized peoples on earth: the Hohokam, archeologists call their old culture. The Hohokam people had small cities, networks of irrigation canals, stone pyramids, a calendar; they were on a level with the pharaonic Egyptians, the Han Chinese. Then something happened—simply a few less inches of rain fell for a few years. Drought burned away the surplus food, and without it Hohokam society could not support pyramids, artists and calendar-keeping technocrat-priests.

Civilization is a luxury, really, a thin skin of gilt on human existence. Strip away the delicate surplus of energy and material that pays for it, and life becomes a matter of bare-bones survival again. The cities vanished; the priests, bards and artisans became extinct. The Hohokam, proud, imperial, gorgeous, became poor, plain, humble Papagos. The canals filled up with dust. What a difference an inch or two of rain makes; on what a frail mist of humidity ride all our dreams of power!

I passed through Papago villages, rancherias really, with such wonderful-sounding names as Ush Kug, Chaiwuli Tak, Wahak Hotrontk. Translated, they have prosaic meanings: "Not Much Water Here," "Lots of Dust," "Pretty Good Place to Grow Beans." Some of the Papago houses were typical Bureau of Indian Affairs constructions, shabby imitations of suburbia. Others, traditional, looked like someone had heaped up shards of dried mud and laid a sheet of rusted iron on top; but the outsides blazed with banks of flowering brush and cacti.

An interesting thing about the Papagos: for centuries, they

have gone south on pilgrimages to the Sea of Cortez, where they gather sea salt on the beaches; the sea is their Mecca, their Lhasa. When Mexico and the United States drew their abstract border across the Papago Nation, the Papagos just kept going on their pilgrimages, sneaking past the border patrol on their ancient trails. The U.S. government accused them of "illegal importation of salt"! Finally, the government gave up; the salt pilgrimages still go on, they say, though the Papagos today have changed a lot since the white men came: they drive pickup trucks, raise cattle and dance to a queer, thumping kind of desert reggae polka called chicken scratch.

I crossed the border at the little town of Sonoyta. The road from Sonoyta west to the delta is a lonesome one, "connecting nothing with nothing." There were dry, deformed mountains on either side of the road, strata frozen in a series of violent epileptic seizures. I passed a crude roadside shrine, a gaudy *santo* staring from behind iron bars. Once in a while, a huge, ponderous Third World truck, painted with Virgins, whores, Orpheuses, angels, *banditos* and clowns, fancy as a mosque, came rolling down the road . . .

About noon I came out of the mountains at San Luis del Colorado, population 63,644. San Luis is a typical small border city, with torn-up streets, tiny shops selling bicycle tires, false teeth, horror comics, fiery black slabs of meat, tiny cloying cakes. The men wore straw cowboy hats, and their faces were long and hard as rawhide. The music on my car radio was all brass and bombast, like a circus marching off to war, and the announcers so splenetic you half expected saliva to come sputtering out of the dashboard. They rolled their r's like castanets.

The whole style of the Frontera is adrenalized and, unsurprisingly, bitter. The Colorado delta area was once a place of Nilotic richness. The Mexican government relocated people from all over the country to live on big, irrigated *ejidos*. It could have been the Imperial Valley of Mexico. But the United States diverted more and more of the water upstream, leaving Mexico with only the flushings of American irrigation—saline,

mineralized. This bad yanqui water poisoned the good Mexican bottomlands and withered the crops. Their own farms
burnt out, the Sonorans were forced to cross the border into
the United States to work on farms irrigated by the very water
they themselves had once owned. Justice is never simple, but
this seemed to me to be a particularly ugly piece of imperialism. Whan a lank, leathery man spat at my car on a back street
of San Luis and shouted *"Puta!"* I wanted to stop and get out
and apologize to him. But my Spanish is bad, and he probably
would not have understood and would have slid a thin, shining
blade, the only bright thing in his life, between my ribs . . .

All that day I searched for the river and its delta, crossing
and recrossing those dank alluvial plains scabbed with desert.
No one I asked seemed to understand what I was looking for:
some pointed north, some south, while one man gestured at the
concrete canal at our feet with the air of a doctor pointing out
the sky to an idiot. Once I came upon a ditch of stale septic
water with a sign that said RIO COLORADO on its banks, but
the water ended a hundred yards downstream, in an embank-
ment.

The air was humid. The land looked like Bengal, patches
green as malachite mingled with ashen hills; California fan
palms sulked in the heat, villages of thatched adobe, hills of
technicolor garbage, here a pig the size of a plow horse, egrets
dozing in the trees, the whole scene compressed under a sky as
slick and hot and heavy as volcanic mud. The back roads were
muck and puddle. Beyond were the peaks of the Baja, the
Sierra los Cocopas, Sierra de la Tinaja, de Juarez, San Pedro
Martir, like crumpled, dusty brown-paper cutouts of mountains.

But where was the river? As the afternoon finally waned, I
drove south, down through Riito, Recuperacion, El Doctor.
There were the railroad tracks I had traveled years ago, par-
alleling the road and then veering off east into the Gran Desierto. Off to the west were swamps, marshes, shoals of mud.
But where was the river Leopold had written about? I feared it
had become nothing more than a spirit, an *espíritu;* and the

jaguars had grown fat and lazy, and gone to the city to be mariachis, blowing bent horns in their gilded coats in the cantinas of San Luis and Mexicali.

That night I read by kerosene lamp in a concrete room in a closed-down hotel in the town of El Golfo de Santa Clara, on the Sea of Cortez. The surf boomed on the beach outside, and the lights of shrimp boats rocked on the black water. "The river does not run to the sea anymore," the old man at the hotel told me. "Isla Montague, Isla Pelican, Isla Gore—all gone now. Mud and sand." I looked over my maps by the sweet yellow light, listening to the winter sea and wondering where I might find a trace of the river—a splinter of metacarpal, a broken syllable of it.

The river I finally found the next afternoon was called the Rio Hardy; it ran along the western edge of the delta, under the dry peaks of the Baja. But it was, a Mexican youth at a roadside cantina assured me, the same as the Colorado. "Rio Hardy, Rio Colorado; Rio Colorado, Rio Hardy," he said, laughing, gesturing out across the brush and water. And so I inflated my little rubber boat, packed it full of gear and headed out onto the slow mulatto waters of the delta.

It was a strange place, acutely schizophrenic. The left bank was wild, impenetrable, with rushes twelve feet high. Leopold had called the delta Pleistocene, but this was Cretaceous, I thought. There were birds everywhere, egrets, cormorants, bitterns, blue herons, green herons striped like cats—feathered serpents, flying reptiles. The silence was broken by their dull croaking and the heavy flapping of their wings as they took off, like someone snapping a wet wool blanket in the mist. There was the silver clatter of coots running on the water on their parchment cymbal feet, flying away downriver low to the water. It was disquieting, all of those ancient plumed beings with their round, cryptic eyes staring at me as I labored down their river.

The right bank, on the other hand, looked like a third-class resort in a nightmare. The brush had been cleared to the ground, and there were vacation homes and cantinas, most of them shuttered down for the winter, bristling with television aerials, with big power boats moored along the shore. A woman in dark glasses and a red bathing suit, lying in a deck chair with a drink in one hand, watched me row past. The only person I met all day on the river was an enormous fat American man in a dinghy with an outboard motor, fishing out in mid-river. He was fishing for bass, and he had the saddest eyes I have ever seen.

"I worked for the Navy in San Diego for forty years," he said. "I own a little house down here, and I come down here to hunt and fish. These camps run way downriver, till the water runs out. They're almost all owned by Americans." He showed me a string of bass, their dead eyes as full of sorrow as his.

I camped that night in a vacant lot between two blocks of vacation homes; there was no place on the east bank I could even go ashore, the brush was so thick.

When I woke the next morning, mariachi music was blaring from a long, golden Buick parked fifty feet away, and a magnificent man in a glossy yellow suit—he was plump and looked as if he had been basted in corn oil—was walking toward me. I crawled out of my sleeping bag and stood up. *"Buenos dias!"* he beamed. "I own all of this land. Actually, there are two hundred lots, and I own twenty-nine and have option on the rest. Soon I will own all! I call this Campo Bebe One, after my daughter, and soon there will be Campo Bebe Two and Three!" I tried to look encouraging. "Pretty soon, big sign on highway, big light! Beer, averything. I no work, I plan!" He almost wriggled with joy. *El hombre dorado,* the gilded man, I thought, looking at him. "I can build you nice house in three days. I also own a construction company. Lotsa American friends living here now. They tell their friends, pretty soon *all* American friends living here!" As I repacked my boat and prepared to push off, he was still talking: "Plenty of time to pay, but you better buy fast. Pretty soon the whole river, *pht!,* sold!" As I rowed down the cold, misting river, he stood there on the bank, waving benevolently, the golden car booming like a giant jukebox.

Instead of getting wilder, the river got worse the deeper I penetrated into the delta. The vacation homes were larger, gaudier. Power boats threshed up and down the river all day, nearly capsizing my little rubber dinghy with their wakes. Worst of all was a kind of skiff with a whole airplane engine and propeller mounted on the rear: you could hear it coming half an hour away, and it literally shook the banks of the river when it passed. Most of the boatsmen were duck hunters, and muffled shotgun volleys echoed constantly, as if there was a little war going on up and down the length of the Rio Colorado delta. "Got forty-four of 'em today," one red-hatted, red-faced thug called out to me as he cruised upriver, one hand on a beer and the other on the wheel of his electric-purple speedboat. I am no foe of hunting: I would rather eat elk than beef, beaver than lamb, rainbows than fish sticks. But the kind of loud, mechanized hunting these men were doing offended me. There was no class, no beauty to it.

By late afternoon I was sick and tired of the river I had dreamt of for so long. It was a long, long way still to the vast mud flats that were all that remained of the heart of the delta, and the way there was little better than a freeway for power boats. I could not see my way to traveling it: it was simply not worth it. The delta was dead and it had left an unbeautiful corpse. I decided to put in on the wild east bank, set up camp and push off into the bush on foot.

Once you pushed through the rushes and thicket that lined the banks, a green strip of jungle perhaps three feet thick, you were abruptly in the desert. Just like that. It was hard to believe you were in the same country at all. Desert stretched away to the jagged horizons.

I lashed my boat to a willow and set up camp in the ruins of a small *campesino* village that had once clung to the river's edge. It was eerie. You could see all the energy, the ingenuity, that had once gone into the place, but it was all dead and gone now. Irrigation ditches crisscrossed the desert, full of nothing: there were fields furrowed, frosted with salt; dry cornstalks poked up, desolate. A brick-lined well went down twenty feet into the hard soil; there was black water at the bottom.

I tried to guess why the people had left. Were they squatters, driven off by some wealthy cattle rancher? Had the fields simply gone bad, scalded dead by the salt in the water? There were ruined houses—hutches, shanties—here and there, and some of them had been burned, the charred hulks of crude furniture still in them. A bed with its gutted mattress still in place sat in the middle of what had once been somebody's bedroom. Somehow this seemed saddest of all to me, thinking of the love that had been made there, the dreams dreamed, the children conceived. It seemed a symbol of the failure of everything most preciously human.

Tribes, villages, families, crack with time, spilling their loose clouds of people out into the world. The great cities inhale these lost people. The farmer who had slept in this slaughtered bed was probably driving a cab in Mexicali now or pushing a shovel in LA. The people were gone, gone forever, leaving this desert of ironwood and thorn, colored like a dried snakeskin or a moth's dusty wing.

I made a circle of crumbling red bricks from one of the houses and built a little fire of thorny sticks. Thunder rolled down out of the mountains of Baja; the air smelled of rain. I set up the tent while the stew simmered on the fire; as I ate, hunched by the smoky fire, the first rain began to flail in on the west wind. It was a strange rain: loud, hard, it didn't really seem to wet anything; the air drank it up even as it struck.

Sitting in the tent, listening to the rain by candlelight, I thought of something funny that had happened to me once on a trip to southern Mexico. I was talking to a thin little fisherman with a pure Indian face: there could hardly have been a drop of Spanish blood in his veins. We were talking about the history of his place, and he told me, very sincerely, "Oh, there used to be many Indians here a long time ago." "Whefe did they go?" I asked. "Oh, they went away somewhere, I guess," he said.

It was the Indians who knew the delta the best, of course: the Cocopahs and the Sand Papagos. As late as the 1930s, the Cocopahs lived in isolated camps in the vast flood plain of the delta, accessible only by foot or horseback in the dry season, dugout canoe in flood time. The Cocopahs hunted desert bighorn, deer, jackrabbits. They worshiped the mountain wildcat (*chimbica,* in the Cocopah tongue). They drank *toloache* (jimsonweed tea) for visions, and traded salt and clamshells to their relatives, the Ipai and Tipai of southern California, for sacred eagle feathers . . . According to the Mexican maps, there are still two Cocopah *ejidos,* cooperative farms, just north of the delta.

The Sand Papagos, then: They lived on the eastern verges of the delta and in the volcanic wastelands of the Pinacates: impossible country. They lived on nothing, made sandals from sea lion hide, ate sand roots, made string from badger hair. According to Charles Bowden's fine book *Killing the Hidden Waters,* the Mexicans and Americans hunted the Sand Papagos to extermination; epidemics finished off the survivors. The last Sand Papago, a hermit named Carvajeles, died around 1912. The Sand Papagos were nomads, Bedouins without camels or tents. They left a few trails from the inland desert to the Sea of Cortez, and grinding stones in caves in the far mountains . . .

The next morning I walked out across that wide, barren plain. It was a chill, windy day, with a keen edge to it, and the sky was gray. An osprey sat in a dead tree holding a big, bloody fish in his claws. I walked and walked on mud roads that led nowhere.

Here and there I came upon more abandoned ranchos, burned huts, ghostly beds. A fancy white 1966 Ford Fairlane without an engine pointed due east, tires gone, parked there forever. I came upon a twisted knot of bobcat shit in the road. Six great, elegant pelicans rode south on the wind toward the sea. Leafless trees, like giant bundles of dead sticks; more burned-down houses, broken bottles, rusted cans. It looked like a war had been fought there and everyone had lost. The roads were heavy with mud; it dragged at my feet, as if it would drag me down under that hopeless country forever.

I felt fear; it stuck in the back of my throat like a numb quid of cocaine. I wanted to run, to run away from those failed farms, those sterile fields, and cross the river and drive north, north to where there were people, green things, red scarves, music; away from this place whose future was interred in salt: Deadland. I had seen enough. I turned and began to follow my steps back, slogging through my own footprints in the leaden mud. I looked up and saw the osprey again.

The osprey hung in the sky on crooked, stabbing wings, hovering over that dead, white country. If there was a message there, and there seemed to be, I did not like the way it read. The Aztecs built their great city of Mexico where an eagle hovered in the sky above the desert, a rattlesnake writhing in its talons. But no one would ever build anything beneath this dark bird; it was an omen of ending.

We live in the aftermath of the Pleistocene, on the dwindling rivulets left over from the Ice Age. Our lands are sore with salt, skinned by the wind, green hills turned on a lathe of drought till the grass and the humus peel away. Apocalypse slides in among us before we know it, quiet as a feeling on the air, a chill in the pit of the belly, a dry lack of dreaming, blue shadows between the ribs of a white horse.

"The rust of your silver, I say, shall eat your flesh as if it were fire," the medieval prophet said. It rang true as a snake's hiss in the silent graveyard of the Colorado.

Or perhaps I just didn't go far enough . . .

On full-moon nights, the Mexicans say, after the spring rains, when the ghost of the river is swollen and cold and the tides are running high, the river reaches the sea again.

The river and the sea rise, black and silver in the moon. A mountain of water rolls in off the Sea of Cortez, drowning the nameless islands, the barren continents of mud and sand: rolls up the channel of the old river in the moonlight. Green herons rise from their nests in the thickets, making music like dull wooden bells . . .

And then the waters turn, and with a tremendous silver noise the river rushes out to sea again, streaming out into the Sea of Cortez.

If you had a boat, the Mexicans say (and I hope they are telling the truth), you could ride all the way from Campo Bebe out to the Sea of Cortez and to the Pacific itself on that black, lunar river.

Barranca del Cobre: The Copper Canyon

FURTHER SOUTH, DOWN THE EAST COAST OF THE SEA OF Cortez, three great rivers flow from the Sierra Madre Occidental: the Rio Yaqui, the Sonora and the Fuerte. If you follow these rivers to their sources, you find yourself in primeval mountains where the old, Indian Mexico still survives.

On the headwaters of the Fuerte (*fuerte* means cold, rainy), tributaries like the Urique, the Oteros and the Batopilas have cut tangled mosaics of gorges, some of them deeper and longer than the Grand Canyon of the Colorado. Along the crest of the Sierra, the thin, burnt, colorless air of the interior, the Great Mexican Desert, like the breath of a giant skeleton, meets the dense, dreamy, moist atmosphere of the Pacific. From the east you gaze off rolling, pine-covered summits into green chasms of swirling mist. It is a true edge, a great divide.

About 40,000 Tarahumara Indians live along these obscure horizons, in isolated caves and rancherias. Like all Indians in Mexico, they are very poor: being Indian in Mexico is a function of money and the style and status that money can buy. Mexico calls itself a *mestizo*, mixed-blood country, but genetically, it is overwhelmingly Indian. A *mestizo* is an Indian with five hundred pesos and a new pair of shoes; a pure Castilian Spaniard of a Mexican is a *mestizo* with a Volkswagen Rabbit and a credit card. Mexico City is full of Indians who are not Indians anymore. The crowds on the subway, with their glossy straight black hair and flat, delicate, impassive faces, look like Olmecs or Toltecs on their way to a pyramid; but all they are now are city Mexicans, landless wage laborers with burned histories and laboriously erased myths, on their way to factory or *futbol* match, movie or mass. People like us. And once you stop being an Indian, you can never go back.

The Tarahumaras are still Indians; like other surviving tribes of Mexico, they live in the steepest, poorest, hardest corner of the landscape. They work corn fields the size of a Persian carpet cut into the side of a mountain. They run down deer on foot till the deer fall over dead from exhaustion. They are the greatest runners on earth: they call themselves *Raramuri*, the Runners, and they run cross-country footraces, kicking little carved hardwood balls twenty or fifty or two hundred miles across the mountains. They are almost constantly inebriated on a native corn brew called *teshuino*, which they spike with jimsonweed or peyotl juice.

There is a wonderful photograph in an old anthropology book whose title I have forgotten that shows a Tarahumara man with a gleeful smile about to pull a cord attached to a stick supporting a slab of stone that must weigh thirty pounds. A tiny wild rodent, something like a coney, is about to hop into the trap. The title of the photograph is "Tarahumara Trapping Wild Game." The photograph is at once ludicrous and profound: the discrepancy between the big rock and the tiny animal is something out of a cartoon; and yet that is how the Tarahumara live, and to them it is deadly serious. You and I would not last long in the Sierra Tarahumara. The Tarahumaras eat wolves, rats, catfish, eels, flies, grasshoppers and worms; toads, lizards, rattlesnakes; juniper berries, wood fungi, cactus fruit, catkins, thirty-nine kinds of wild weed; thirteen varieties of roots. They raise cattle, pigs, sheep and goats, mostly for the wool and the manure (for fertilizer). They grow corn, bean and squash on cobblestone ground. Since 1607, when the first Jesuit missionaries came into the Tarahumara country, followed by slave-taking Spanish silver miners and ranchers, the Tarahumaras have had to fight fiercely to maintain their tight, risky way of life. The Mexicans call the most Tarahumara of the Tarahumaras *cimmarones*—the wild ones.

Some say the Tarahumaras still have wizards, *brujos*. There are accounts of whole mountains lighting up in the night like lanterns, switched on by a crowd of Tarahumaras roaring an incantation. Who knows? The country and the people are wild enough for anything. There are pumas in the eastern Sierra,

jaguars in the barrancas. The last of the giant Sonoran griz-
zlies, if there are any left at all, live on the highest mountains.
The Mexican government maps of the area (*Estados Unidos
Mexicanos*, 1:250,000) are highly imaginative. The most
famous book about the country, *Les Tarahumaras*, was written
by Antonin Artaud at the Hôpital Psychiatrique in Aveyron,
France. Artaud visited the Sierra Tarahumara in 1936, but
Les Tarahumaras is more about the paranoid, ecstatic topog-
raphy of Artaud's mind than about the sierra and the barrancas
of the Tarahumara. Trying to find your way around the Sierra
Madre Occidental using Artaud's book is like trying to find out
about Kansas by reading *The Wizard of Oz*. There is one great
passage in *Les Tarahumaras*, though, that conveys, perhaps
inadvertently, the immense splendor and loneliness of the Sierra Madre: "Man is alone, desperately scraping out the music
of his own skeleton, without father, mother, family, love, god
or society . . . And one walks from the equinox to the solstice,
buckling on one's own humanity."

In 1966 a friend and I took a Volkswagen with 195,000 miles
on it south into Mexico, from Juarez to Durango, across to
Mazatlan and north up the coast to Nogales. It was my first trip
to Mexico, and we traveled along the very outer edge of the
Tarahumaras and their mountains.

We saw bands of Indians along the highway, on pilgrimage to
gather peyotl; and in the Park in Durango we met a spooky
guy, a dead ringer for Humphrey Bogart, who said he had been
prospecting for gold in the Sierra Madre. "Oh, it's back there
all right," he said, squinting and chewing on a cigarette. "They
never did find the mother lode." His Sierra was a country of
bald lies: of glittering ice mountains, of gorges choked with
snow, of pumas as big as bulls screaming in the night. Later we
crossed the Sierra Madre just south of the Tarahumara
country on the Durango-Mazatlan road: eerie country, fog-
shrouded, with shack towns on the mountainsides and huge
lumber trucks lit like *fata morgana* looming in the darkness.

A few years later I returned, in winter, with another old car, and tried to drive from Chihuahua City to Estacion Creel, in the barranca country. The car got stuck in a river west of Cuahtemoc and I continued on by train. The train left Cuah- temoc two hours late, and ten minutes out of La Junta some- thing in the engine exploded, starting a brushfire that raged across the blanched tinder hills to the horizon. The passengers sat and watched the fire like a crowd at a circus, exclaiming happily as isolated trees went up in puffs of flame, whooshes of sudden combustion; they munched tacos and drank beer. In the late afternoon another engine was brought out from Cuah- temoc, and we continued up into the Sierra Madre.

Dusk gathered; the air outside turned cold. We chugged up a river valley, through timber, past tiny muddy villages of split logs and stone. There was snow on the ground here and there. Whenever the train stopped, the lights in the coaches went out and we were plunged into darkness. We stopped at one starlit village, and when the lights went on again there was an Indian sitting on the wooden bench opposite me. Our knees nearly touched. He stared at me as if utterly amazed. He was not a Tarahumara; I don't know what he was. He wore a rough white cotton shirt and pants, and a broad-brimmed sombrero hung with feathers from unimaginable birds. His feet, in bro- ken leather sandals, looked like they had been walking around the world since the beginning of time. The whites of his eyes were yellow. He kept one big gnarled hand on a burlap bundle next to him. He kept staring at me. At the next village the lights went out again, and when they went on he was gone.

I spent a few days at Estacion Creel, roaming the country- side around the town. A large concrete Jesus spread his arms from the cliffs above the town. There were no Tarahumaras living in Creel, but the country around the town was full of their farms and corrals, in clearings in the forest and clefts in the rock. The Indians stared at me in silence as I passed, waiting for me to go away. They were short people, wild and clear-eyed. At night I drank with a mournful Yaqui Indian named Gomez who looked exactly like the French comedian

Fernandel, at a bar and bordello called the Amor y Indio ("Love and the Indian"). The girls were mountain Indians from lost, distant tribes, and they carried daggers in their stockings. The mescal tasted like turpentine and made you crazy. Late at night, wolves or wild dogs howled in the hills.

The heart of the Sierra Tarahumara is the Barranca del Cobre, the Copper Canyon, part of the Rio Urique gorge; it is the longest, deepest canyon in the Tarahumara country. The Copper Canyon got its name from the copper mines, now abandoned, on its headwaters. *Urique* is a Tarahumara word: it has several different meanings, but in this case it probably derives from *uri,* meaning grapevine and referring to the sinuous course of the river.

Some geographers have called the Copper Canyon the deepest in the world, but it isn't, really. The Tarahumara barrancas do not fall away in a single, dramatic plunge, the way the Grand Canyon of the Colorado does; they are more gradual, a series of tilted cliffs, rifts, titanic rubble staircases with gorges at the bottom. What the barrancas *are* is the most extensive, least explored, most *confused* maze of chasms on earth. The Copper Canyon is only a small piece of the puzzle: down a thousand feet; across a broken plateau; down another twenty-five hundred feet; out onto a ribbon of a ridgeline, step one way and you fall two thousand feet into one river, step the other and you fall two thousand feet into another river. You could lose a dozen Grand Canyons in those stone convolutions.

A winter or two ago, I drove down to Mexico again, bound for the Barranca del Cobre. I was with a Mexican-American friend from Los Angeles with the unlikely name of Max Hoffmanstahl. The weather was cold and cloudy when we left Ciudad Juarez. We traveled south through the Great Desert: dunes, violet brush, fantastic stone mountains; a landscape off the cover of a Castaneda book. I counted five kinds of hawk in ten miles. At Chihuahua City we turned west; the road began to climb slowly through Cuahtemoc, La Junta. We came to a

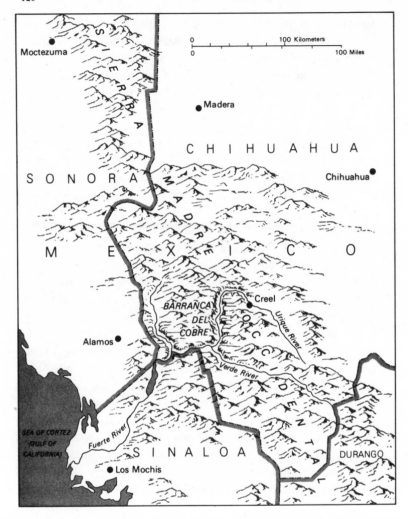

little guard post along the road about nightfall, one of those weird paramilitary checkpoints you run into in Mexico. A man in a khaki greatcoat, an assault rifle on his back, came out of the little adobe shack and looked us over. "We're going to Creel," we said. He shrugged and went back inside.

The pavement ended and we drove on over rocks and deep ruts. We crossed steep timbered valleys and drove through shallow rivers. Here and there were tiny kerosene-lit hamlets, dim and golden as *candelarias*. We drove and drove. The air was sharply cold and the trees were big now: ponderosa, Mexican pine, Engelman spruce, aspen.

Around midnight we found ourselves driving through the clouds into the town of San Juanita, on the railroad line into Creel, the same line I had ridden ten years ago. It was a logging town; big stacks of green lumber, glittering with frost, cured by the side of the road, a sweet, dank smell. It was only twenty miles to Creel, the jumping-off point for the Barranca del Cobre, but we were too exhausted to go on. The fog was so thick you could barely see beyond the hood of the car. It had taken us seven hours to drive the seventy-odd miles from La Junta on those calamitous roads. We drove through town, wallowing in potholes full of ice and water. Finally we came to a hotel with an iconic light burning. On a table in the lobby was a stuffed river otter two and a half feet long, and a gaunt Indian in a knit skullcap slept on a wooden cot. The Indian woke up, looked at us and groaned. He led us upstairs to a windowless room painted brilliant turquoise and lit by a bare light bulb: forty pesos, two dollars. It was nearly as cold inside the hotel as out. Max and I unrolled our sleeping bags on the hard cots. I bought a bottle of lukewarm grapefruit soda from the Indian, drank it and slid halfway into an uneasy sleep.

The next morning we left our car in Creel and walked south out of town. A Jesuit priest in Creel, Father Luis Verplancken, had told us of a trail through the main gorge of the Urique: Walk out of town on the road to La Bufa two or three miles, and you will see a river running west; follow the river into the canyon and walk for three days; then ask a Tarahumara for directions to Divisadero. Climb eighteen miles, 7,000 vertical feet, up the north side of the canyon to Divisadero. Catch the train back to Creel (there should be one in a couple of days, at the most).

The problem was, we could not find the way. We walked and walked down the rock-strewn dirt road, lugging our packs, studying our Mexican topo map and searching for the priest's river. Tarahumaras watched us from their wooden shanties. The sky was dim blue, smudged with cloud. The weather was changing: you could feel it in the air, wintry, flinty, disturbing. There was no sign of a westward-running river anywhere; a dry creek bed ran back toward Creel and disappeared. Max asked directions from an Indian man chopping wood in a field. The man looked at us blankly for a long time, waiting for us to disappear. "I don't know!" he finally said in Spanish, and went back to chopping wood. We started off down the road again. It wound away into the distance before us, through timber, cliffs, sere winter pasture. There was no sign at all of the priest's river, or of the deepest canyon on earth.

Finally, we sat down by the road and studied the map again. Forty miles south, we discovered, the road we were on actually *crossed* the canyon of the Rio Urique. The canyon wasn't as deep there as it was between Creel and Divisadero, where the priest had directed us, but it looked even wilder. There was no railroad, and the only settlements on the map were Tarahumara rancherias like Umirao, Rancho Napuchic, Basiguate, Guahuachique.

A few minutes later we flagged down two Mexican loggers in a battered pickup truck and were heading south for the bridge across the Barranca del Cobre, forty miles away across a tangled maze of mountains and arroyos. According to the map, we were skirting the eastern edge of the Continental Divide. The streams we crossed fed into the Rio Concho, the River of Shells, which flowed northeast across the Great Chihuahuan Desert into the Rio Grande. Just over the ridges to the west were the canyons of the Rio Urique. The Urique ran north and then southwest, joining the Rio Fuerte, the River of Cold Rain; the Fuerte crossed the coastal deserts of Sinaloa and entered the Sea of Cortez just north of Los Mochis. Late that after-noon, after three long, slow truck rides through the mountains, we came at last to the Barranca del Cobre.

The truck drove away. Far below the concrete bridge, the white water of the Rio Urique lashed and boiled in the rock. We walked back up the road till we found a way down, and clambered down a steep slope of stones, brambles and dust to the canyon floor.

"To visit the Tarahumara is to enter a world which is in-credibly anachronistic and exists in defiance of this age," Ar-taud wrote; down here the madman's words seemed to be true. We were at the bottom of a gorge about 1,500 feet deep. Gray igneous cliffs rose on either side, broken by weird tangled forests of pine and oak, mountain mahogany, clumps of prickly pear, spindly yuccas as tall as the mast of a small ship.

It looked something like certain canyons in southeastern Utah, the country around Cigarette Springs Cave or the wrong side of the Blue Mountains, I thought. Then I changed my mind: it looked like the tangled, overgrown hills of Nepal. It looked like a Chinese landscape scroll, one of those delicate gorges that unravels to the cloudy edge of the void. It looked like the impossible country in a painting on a Mexican calen-dar, with Aztec pyramids perched on the tops of jungle moun-tains, vaporous rock towers, technicolor jungles.

We started down the canyon. There were Indian trails, overgrown, through the thickets. We picked our way through the boulders at the river's edge. In places where the water was waist-deep, we had to wade the river, which was surprisingly cold. If we had had an inflatable kayak, or even a truck-tire inner tube, we could have floated the river with ease, but on foot our progress was slow.

That was all right: it gave us plenty of time to see things. We came upon recently painted pictographs on the cliffs, rough ruby-red daubings of stick men, deer with tremendous antlers like upside-down chandeliers, sheep and goats: the latest thing in Stone Age art. We passed a Tarahumara storehouse, a sealed turret of stone and adobe three feet high and two feet across, probably full of dry corn brought down from the mesas. There were animal signs everywhere in the sand and gravel along the river—deer; the dexterous paw prints of ringtail cats (hordes of them) and, in one spot, the tracks of an eagle, the claws as big as my hand.

At dusk, about three miles down from the bridge, we made camp. I gathered driftwood—perfect snow-white sticks as dry and light as Styrofoam—and built a fire. The river rumbled by on its cobbled bed. We ate sausage and sour Mexican cheese and lemonade heavily dosed with iodine to kill off the hepatitis bacilli and sheep-liver flukes in the crystal-clear water.

Just as the sun went down, we heard a wordless cry from high on the rim; we looked up, and there was a lone Indian, dressed in white, waving his arm slowly, majestically against the sky. We waved back. The Indian vanished, and a few moments later we heard the cry again and saw the same Indian waving to us from a point a half-mile distant from where we had first seen him. The Indian vanished again; and again, a few moments later, he reappeared impossibly far away on the rimrock, calling to us, waving against the evening sky. His voice rang plaintively down the chasm. What he was—phantom, *brujo* or a team of Tarahumara tricksters who specialize in fooling *gringo* travelers—we could not guess.

The first stars appeared through a thin, wet scud of clouds. Bats sailed low over the river, twisting and turning in the twilight.

The next morning we headed down canyon again.

According to the map, it was almost fifty miles to the deepest part of the Barranca del Cobre, below Divisadero. We didn't really hope to get that far: from what we had heard, there was no way of traveling that fifty miles in less than ten days. There were overhanging runoffs and places where the riverbanks vanished into sheer cliffs: you had to swim or float for miles, your pack lashed to your back. So we had heard. There was no way of knowing. In the rainy season, the Rio Urique is totally impassable, raging with debris-choked flood waters. In the heart of the dry season you could travel for miles without finding enough water to fill your boot. Hiking across bone-dry boulders, Max and I looked up and saw huge driftwood logs caught in the cliff ten feet over our heads.

We had enough food for five or six days and a map that might have been drawn by a drunken pilot looking down on the country through broken clouds. What did we care? *Cimmarones,* we wandered through the brilliant abyss.

Laboring our way west by northwest down canyon, we kept our eyes out for Tarahumaras. We didn't see any that day, but their traces were everywhere: crude stone corrals in shallow caves; bare footprints in the sand (great splayed feet); peeled logs left in the rocks. We heard goat bells, the braying of flocks, from high on the canyon walls. All around us, above us, the Raramuri were cutting firewood, drinking *teshuino,* sawing away on hand-hewn violins, plowing their tiny aeries of field. What we were traveling through was a human wilderness, a country where man still lived out his life in a prehuman world of clouds and lions, famine and stone. There are few such places left on earth, eddies in the oily rip tide of history.

It would be a mistake to romanticize the Tarahumaras. Their lives are hard, harder than we can imagine. Their heartland is crumpled and corrugated till there is hardly enough flat space to lie down in: villages and farms hang by the fingernails over thin air. Their shanties are full of smoke, their dwarf corn is shot full of worms, and their *teshuino* gives them dysentery; when they are sober they are gloomy; when they are drunk, which is most of the time, they argue, fight and seduce each other's wives. Their god is Onoruame, a sinister deity who causes floods, sickness, disease, death. Hard lives, hard deaths. I would not want to be a Tarahumara.

Still, it is that very harshness that gives the Runners their power. Living the way they do, it is no wonder they can run two hundred miles on a bellyful of corn brew; no wonder they can turn stone mountains to light with their singing, and flit over the rimrock like sparrow hawks. In the Sierra, only magicians survive.

I quote from a wonderful book called *Peyote Hunt,* by the anthropologist Barbara Meyerhoff. Dr. Meyerhoff spent several years with the Huichols, who live south of the Tarahumaras in the mountains around Guadalajara. One day a shaman named Ramon Medina Silva led Dr. Meyerhoff and a group of Huichols to a precipice, "a steep barranca, cut by a rapid waterfall cascading perhaps a thousand feet over jagged, slippery rocks. At the edge of the fall Ramon removed his sandals and told us that this was a special place for shamans. We watched in astonishment as he proceeded to leap across the waterfall, from rock to rock, pausing frequently, his body bent forward, his arms spread out, his head thrown back, entirely birdlike . . . We outsiders were terrified and puzzled but none of the Huichols seemed at all worried."

You learn something new every day: the next day we learned never to buy canned salmon in Mexico. Our can with the iridescent sockeye leaping on the label turned out to contain lumps of pale, pulpy Mystery Fish, with enough salt to preserve a pharaoh and enough oil to lubricate a Mexican logging truck for a year. We ate our last two oranges and a handful of Animalitas for breakfast, washed down with more iodine-spiked lemonade.

We walked on under low, dismal skies. There were coyote tracks in the sand and ringtail cat tracks, studded with berries, everywhere.

Again, I found myself thinking of Asia: more than anything else, the Sierra Tarahumara was like a little piece of Nepalese hill country that had drifted loose and somehow come to rest between Chihuahua City and Navajoa, in a blank part of Mexico. There were the same endless river valleys separated by steep, forested ridgelines; the same scenes of green vegetation and gray sky; even the Tarahumaras, if you didn't look too hard, could have been Gurungs or Tamangs—squat, lithe hill people trotting forever across the jade ravines and mountains. A primeval world.

The hike was not easy. The river had cut a lovely, precipitous series of flumes and waterfalls in the rose-colored stone. We had to scramble around on the cliffs above plunge pools of icy water, or bushwhack across the steep forests above the inner gorge. The trails through the forest were probably the equivalent of interstate highways to the Tarahumara, but for us they were slow going. They faded out into networks of deer trails that dead-ended in the middle of nowhere or wound up through brittle rock bands and then vanished into luxuriant groves of poison ivy. There is nothing more discouraging than slipping on a disintegrating boulder, grabbing onto a branch to keep from falling, and finding yourself with a death grip on a damp, shining clump of trinary leaves. It was obvious that we would never make it to Divisadero; that, in fact, our alternative plan of hiking down to the abandoned Spanish silver mine at the mouth of the Rio Asararo and hiking back to the road via the Asararo gorge was also impossible. We would have to try and find a way to climb and bushwhack our way out of this maze of cliffs, and then try and find our way back up to the road.

Late that afternoon we made camp by the river. As dusk moved up the canyon, a Tarahumara came jogging down through the timbered mountainside to the south. He was carrying a big bundle of sugarcane over one shoulder and leading three little pack mules loaded with heavy burlap bundles. A tiny dog—it looked like a cross between a fox and a coyote—trotted along behind. We walked upstream to meet him.

He watched us approach with an inscrutable expression on his face. He was an old man; a thin, small man, his long hair streaked with colors of ash, iron. His face was mapped with deep furrows, as if he carried an impression of the barranca country stamped across his physical being. He wore a native shirt and a pair of slick brown polyester pants, and there was a rucksack on his back, supported by a rope to a kind of cloth-covered collar around his head. He was barefoot; he carried a pair of dilapidated *huaraches* stuffed in his pockets.

His name was Manuel Ortega, he said; and he had started out the day before from the town of Urique, about a hundred miles away at the other end of the Tarahumara country. He had bartered a load of oranges in Urique and was taking it back to the high country to trade for something else. He was from Yahuirachic, about twenty miles south of Creel; he would be home the next morning, he said. He laughed suddenly. "My home is in the mountains," he said. The thought pleased him evidently, and he laughed again.

I tried to imagine the hundred miles of country he had crossed in the last day and a half: boulder fields, cliffs, traverses over smoking waterfalls, brush-choked ravines, steep timber . . . It was impossible. Of course, the Indian on the cliff had been impossible too. A highly trained American or European marathon runner with mountaineering experience just might have been able to keep up with the old man for a day—maybe. But not barefoot, bent under a rucksack, with a bundle of cane over one shoulder and a pack train to keep in line. No, it was impossible.

I found myself thinking of Milarepa, the eleventh-century Tibetan hermit who crossed the Himalayas in midwinter with nothing but a thin cotton robe and a begging bowl. The old Indian was like that. He stood there, a bemused expression on his face, as if he was waiting for us to do something.

On an impulse I reached into my pocket, took out a couple of peso coins, worth about ten cents each, and held them out to him. The impossible old man broke into a beautific smile, took the coins, jingled them in his hand and started up the trail again, followed by his mules and his little fox-colored dog, up into the vast canyon walls. We heard him laughing to himself as he trudged up the trail.

One time in India I got drunk with a lama of the "crazy

wisdom" school of Tibetan Buddhism. This was in Dharamsala, a Tibetan village 7,000 feet up in the Himalayas of Mimachal Pradesh. The lama had long hair, a wispy beard and mustache, and he carried a human-skullcap drinking bowl and a bone rosary under his russet robes. He was almost deaf and very nearly blind; he looked like an old benevolent tiger.

We drank and drank kettleful after kettleful of *chung,* the potent beer of the Himalayas, far into the night. Sometime after midnight the old wizard decided he wanted to go home to the village below. The hut where the party had been going on was a couple of miles above Dharamsala, and it was raining hard outside; the only way down was a steep, slippery trail that wound through the jungle.

The Tibetan lady who owned the house tried to argue the old lama out of going, but he insisted; so she went in the back room, found a lantern and gave it to him to light his way. He thanked her profusely, drank a last cup of *chung,* bowed to us all and went out into the night carrying the lantern, which he had neglected to light, in front of him. Blind, drunk, carrying a dark iron box to illuminate the trail, the crazy, wise old lama vanished down the steep mountain trail as easily as if he were strolling a sidewalk in broad daylight.

Clambering over gnarled boulders, picking our way through the seething waters, we traveled downriver. At the rate we were going, I figured we would reach the plains of Sinaloa in about a month and a half; and in about two months we would be in Los Mochis, eating giant shrimp broiled with garlic and drinking Pacifico beer ("*Pacifico, y nada mas!*" the ads say). It was a long, long way to go. Supposedly the Rio Urique and the Rio Fuerte had never been traveled from source to mouth, and I could see why.

The canyon was too beautiful, and I found myself wondering how long it would last. The night before, camped in a place that looked like it hadn't changed in a hundred thousand years—boulders, river, forest, bats twisting through the campfire smoke—a light flashed high in the distant rimrock, and we saw the faint headlight beams of a logging truck, heard the low rumble of the motor as it hauled another load of logs, another piece of the Sierra Tarahumara, away. Someday, no doubt, there will be dams on these wild rivers, holding the white water back; the Tarahumaras will give up their lonely, brave lives and drift down out of the mountains to the cities on the plains. They will forget their very name, *Raramuri*.

Like redwoods, brown bears, white water and green mountains, the Tarahumaras belong to the end of the Ice Age, the great birthing of flora, fauna, language, myth, that swarmed across the Americas, ebbed and has now shrunk to a few remote pockets, middens: Barranca del Cobre, Cerro Pincate, the Snake Mountains, Paoha Island . . . It flickers, echo of an echo of a ghost-dance song.

The morning of the last day, we hiked out of the gorge in a cold, relentless drizzle.

As we climbed, the canyon country opened up below. The south fork of the Urique rolled on, picking up the Asararo and a dozen other tributaries before it met the main gorge of the Urique somewhere in the hazy distance. Beyond the canyons of the Urique, to the north, were the canyons of the Sepentrion and the Oteros, which joined the Rio Fuerte at the western edge of the Sierra. To the south were the Rio Verde and the Rio Chinatu, two more major tributaries of the Urique, more tangled, cloudy gorges; and beyond, somewhere, the Rio Sinaloa. Looking down on it all, I felt as if the slightest wind would lift me, a disembodied spirit, into the raining skies and out over the hollowed sierra.

We crossed a high, timbered hill and left the canyons behind. We descended into a stark valley. There was a Tarahumara rancheria there: stone-walled fields of corn stubble, split-log shanties and barns, a chicken coop on stilts. Cattle and sheep grazed in the fields. Women in gypsy red watched us from behind a wall. Wood smoke oozed from the roofs. A gaggle of raggedy children pointed to us, whispering to each other. The whole village couldn't have been bigger than ten, twelve acres. There, right there, on a patch of stricken stony ground with a thread of stream winding through it, two dozen people lived their lives. How? It seemed impossible. But there they were, the Raramuri, smiling at us as we tramped through their tiny hardscrabble village. It was the poorest village in the world. A man pounding maguey with a huge wooden mallet (the crushed maguey would be used to make beer) stopped to wave to us; he was laughing delightedly.

A few minutes later we were on the road. A Mexican in a Ford pickup stopped, and then we were riding in the dust and snow swirling down now out of that ancient country, green as corroded copper, carved by the silver knives of the rivers; where bats rule over the night and ravens rule the day, and every man is in his heart a *cimmarone,* consumed by beauty and by loneliness.

Dead Seas and Diggers: The Great Basin

BEYOND THE COLORADO PLATEAU, OUT IN THE EERIE DRY lakes, nightmare mountains and charnel rivers of central Utah, the Great Basin begins. Traveling west to California on old Highway 40, you know you are there when you pass Sevier Lake, just before Deadman's Pass, and the Snake Mountains of Nevada. Sevier Lake is an alkaline dust bowl, almost pewter in the smudgy, dusty light, with a few pockets of bitter water here and there. Dust devils saraband across the salt flats; beyond lie the hopeless white sepulchers of the Beaver Mountains. It is one of the most dreadful landscapes on earth, kin in its fearsomeness to the Dasht-i-Margo of Afghanistan and certain parts of the Chihuahuan Desert.

From Sevier to the eastern edge of the Sierra Nevada, you are in the Great Basin—Digger country. The early white explorers and historians called the Indians of the Great Basin "Diggers" because they dug for roots and grubs and ate brine-fly larvae and crickets in order to survive. It was a term of contempt. The historian H. H. Bancroft described the Basin Indians this way: "Lying in a state of semi-torper in holes in the ground during winter, and in spring crawling forth and eating grass on their hands and knees, until able to regain their feet; having no clothes, scarcely any cooked food, in many cases no weapons, with only a few vague imaginings for religion, lying in the utmost squalor and filth, putting no bridle on their passions, there is surely room for no missing link between them and the brutes." Fool Bancroft: he should have tried surviving without steel, powder, machine-woven cloth for a month or a week—four days and nights—out in that terrible country.

What the Basin Indians were, of course, Bancroft could not understand: they were master omnivores, almost supernatural survivors, able to pull rabbits out of non-existent hats, conjure houses out of a few armloads of dead reeds, find water in a sea of dusty stones. Digger tribes like the Piutes, Goshiutes and Washoes lived in the most barren niches of the Basin, places where Bancroft would have died in a day or two. There were Indian tribes in the awful mountains above Sevier Lake and in Death Valley (a small band still lives there); in Panamint Basin, Skull Valley, the Black Rock Desert, the flats around Great Salt Lake. It was a civilization of the highest sophistication: sleek, flexible, incredibly adaptable and almost infinitely portable.

The white reaction to all this was typified by Bancroft and is typical of Western man's reaction to energy-poor peoples: they are "unpeople," less than human, and as such, they are fair game. The pioneer whites of the Basin used to go "Indian-hunting" on weekends just as they go "varmint-hunting" today: dead counted more than wounded, and adults more than children. As late as the 1910s, a band of Piutes—men, women and children—were slaughtered by whites in western Nevada: they had been forced off of their land by encroaching settlers, were starving to death and stumbled on some range cattle, which they killed and butchered in order to survive. The whites called them rustlers and killed every one of them without a trial.

Perhaps what the whites in the Basin felt toward the land and its people was less condescension than mystification, and fear. How did people live out there, anyway, without gunpowder and iron, wells and wheels and grease? There was a kind of black magic to it: the technology of the Basin Indians was so alien to settlers as to resemble a sort of dry voodoo. Shakespeare, after all, modeled Caliban on reports from the New World of "Indians"; and strangest of the strange were these quiet, obdurate basin people who chose to live in the worst, most stringent part of the great American desert.

Their survival, we now know, was based on a delicate, preternatural understanding of the seasonal tides of seed, nut, root, bug and rodent in the microenvironments that make up the Basin. One month they were netting jackrabbits in a foothill meadow; the next, harvesting pine nuts in a piñon forest

high on a mountainside in one of the ranges—the Rubies,
Skulls, Snakes—that rise like atolls from the floor of the Basin;
later in the year they might be hunting migrating birds on one
of the alkali lakes that stripe the desert.

Unlike the desert Indians of the Southwest, who learned to
farm from the Indians of Mexico, the Basin people never had
agriculture to lean on; and they never became "horse Indians,"
mounted warriors and hunters, as did their neighbors to the
north and east. It was strictly a matter of environment. Outside
the Basin, for instance, in the wetter, grassier prairies of Idaho
and Washington and Wyoming, Shoshoni bands became
plains-style, horseback nomads; while in the rainless Basin
there was not enough grass to feed a horse herd on, and no
game big enough to make mounted hunting worthwhile. If a
Basin Shoshoni found a stray Spanish, Anglo, or Indian horse,
he did not ride it; he shot it and ate it. And as far as farming was
concerned, there were no great river systems, such as the Rio
Grande, the Colorado and the San Juan, that could support
agriculture. The Basin people were doomed to a life of meticu-
lous scavenging, of rag-and-bone picking raised to a high art.
And what they did not have, they traded for: there was an
elaborate commerce through the Great Basin, both east and
west—obsidian and brine-fly pupae cakes exported in ex-
change for acorns, furs, salmon.

This kind of life, which our early, arrogant historians saw as
low and beastly, was actually one of subtle grace and sophistication. I once saw a film by Norman Tinsdale, the great, ec-
centric Australian anthropologist, that laid bare the beauty of
hunting and gathering at its most intense. A lone aborigine
man, utterly naked, was wandering across a hardpan desert.
He sighted a tiny, stingless Australian desert bee and gave
chase; he followed it for miles, loping along, till he came to a
huge dead tree. The bee vanished somewhere high up in the
trunk. The aborigine, in a few easy motions, seized a sharp
cobble from the ground, shinnied up the smooth trunk, somehow found the tiny hole that marked the bee's hive and hacked
off a piece of bark to serve as a dish; dug out the whole bee

hive—honey, wax, larvae and all—and scooped it into his bark dish; then slid down the tree and proceeded to eat the whole sweet, living, golden mass with his long black fingers, smiling shyly at the camera as he did so. It was a lovely film: it could have been a ballet of hunger, the hunt and satisfaction. In our obsession with artifacts, we miss much that is graceful and fine in human ways.

I first really got to know the basin in the early 1970s, when Gordon Wiltsie, a climbing friend, invited me to visit him in Bishop, California, where the basin meets the eastern Sierra Nevada. Until that time, the basin had always been a kind of big interruption between Colorado and California, a geographic purgatory to me. From a speeding car (and you drive as fast as you can) the landscape looks dull: the sullen hills, the endless repetition of sagebrush sagebrush sagebrush, rabbit-brush, bitterbrush, coyotebrush. On the passes they call summits, the trees are scrub, barely head high. Here and there where someone has tried to mine is a hummock of corrosion, yellow, ocher. In the distance mountains, snowy in the winter, float like shrouds. The cities—Las Vegas, Reno, Winnemucca, Sparks, Lovelock and the rest—are convulsions of febrile activity: the kind you find in a maze full of rats fed on cocaine-infused nutrients.

Gordon was born and raised in the Owens Valley, on the rim of the basin; and through him (as a mountaineer, he was in peculiarly close contact with the terrain), I began to see something of the land as it really was. That Shoshoni garage mechanic with a bear-claw necklace was a medicine man in his spare time. There was an old, old man who lived in a tarpaper shack in Poverty Hills and who looked like a tramp but was really a coyote doctor. "You drive around with him in the middle of the day," the local Indians said, "and you see coyotes everywhere." Years ago, when he was young, he fasted on a mountaintop above the Fish Lake Valley in Nevada—fasted until a coyote came, lay down beside him and spoke to him. In the coldest, loneliest part of the night, they talked together. Now coyotes follow him everywhere. They run in broad daylight in front of his truck, they lie on his roof for the heat in the winter. "Hell," said a young Indian, "that old man could call up a hunnert coyotes in downtown New York, I bet."

The old Indians will not touch iron to their hair, or to the meat they eat; instead of knives, they use long flaked-obsidian blades—thin, almost invisible when turned on edge, with a rainbow of black colors dancing inside. When they get sick, they go to the sweat lodge. Some of them will still not ride in a car or truck. Instead, they *walk* along the highway from one town to another, thirty, forty miles in this deserted country. These are stubborn folk.

Late that summer was the Annual Pow-wow and Indian Rodeo in Bishop; and Indians came from all over the Great Basin and beyond to attend—from such places as the Smoke Creek Desert and White Swan, Smith Valley and Fish Lake Valley, Mud Sea and Pyramid Lake, as well as Phoenix, Los Angeles, Albuquerque, Red Deer, Canada. There were not only Piutes, Shoshonis and the related Uto-Aztecan Basin people; there were Colvilles and Yakimas, Tules and Modocs from across the Sierra, and Pit River people from the lava country far to the north; Yakimas, Choctaws and Sioux from LA; even Mission Indians from the tiny remnant bands in the southern California desert. They had gathered to ride in the rodeo, to feast, to gamble, to drink and dance, and to be together. For there are few Indians left in America—a bare million out of our 250-odd million—and gatherings of Native Americans in such numbers, in one place at one time, give some feeling of comfort, of warmth. Bishop is a town of 30,000, and about 4,000 of these people are Bishop Piutes, living mostly on the western edge of town in something between a neighborhood and a reservation. It was hard to count, but there must have been at least 10,000 Indian visitors from out of town at the pow-wow that year. To the crowds there, it must have been glorious, a reprieve from the cold, gray America we have built on top of the continent they call Turtle Island.

There were slick Reno Indians with big mustaches and blow-dried hair, wearing doubleknit slacks, prismatic cowboy shirts (one had an air-brushed painting of a pool cue and balls in full color on the back), Tony Lama snakeskin boots. There were old, gnarled mountain Indians from the ranges behind Fallon, Hiko, Battle Mountain, with scorched skin and milky eyes, leaning on wooden staffs like the sages in an Oriental scroll, cocking their ears to the foreign sound of English. There were big dire-looking toughs just out of prison ("What did you do?" "Manslaughter. Two counts"), swaggering with cases of beer under their arms, drinking them down and tossing the empty bottles off into the crowd. There were young girls with a taut, almost angry, epicanthic beauty, their hair long and loose. There were white-haired, sunny-faced matrons in gingham dresses, eating fry bread. There were children, plump and bright as topaz.

The rodeo was like any other small-town rodeo, except that the contestants and the crowd were all Indians. The National American Indian Rodeo Cowboy Association circuit goes on all summer and into the fall, from Gu Oidak to Medicine Hat. The announcer, who shouted in a perfect Anglo cowboy drawl, but who may, after all, have been an Indian (cultural ironies abound out here: Indian cowboys, redskin rednecks), cracked a string of dusty jokes: "How do you get to be a bull rider?" No answer. "Put seven rubber balls in your mouth an' spit one out every day—and when you ain't got any balls left, you're a bull rider!" A ripple of laughter and shouts of derision came from the crowd. "How do you tell an Indian streaker?" he yelled. "By his high cheeks!" Scattered applause. "What's the difference between a snowman and a snowwoman?" This time someone in the crowd shouted before he could answer himself—"Snowballs!"—and the crowd cheered wildly. But the rodeo itself was nothing much: the stock were average, the ropers and riders no better than most.

What was remarkable were the faces in the crowd and the

mountains rising on both sides, east and west of the town: the White Mountains, the color of nothing, where the oldest living things in the world are—bristlecone pines *(Pinus longaeva)*, born 4,500 years ago and still alive*; and the eastern Sierra Nevada, knobbled and carved and cuneiformed with gray ice, dirty snow. We might have been in a valley in Tibet or Mongolia: the dryness, the mountains, the brown faces, eager, smiles gleaming, and the clothes of many colors, the delight in primary colors.

That night Gordon and I drove out to the Bishop Indian Center, in the cottonwoods down by the Owens River, for the hand game. The Indians own one whole side of Bishop, and it is interesting and enlightening to see what they have done with it. Almost nothing: they have left it alone. Anglo Bishop is all motels, gas stations, stores, restaurants, apartments; Indian Bishop is a patchwork of little farms, groves of trees, creeks wending through, a few horses and cattle grazing. The Indian town is less a town than a tract of little farms and land left rough, unused.

The hand game is a particularly rich cultural artifact, an amalgam of gambling, ritual, song cycle, social gathering and show of power; and today it also functions as a kind of confirmation of Indian-ness, a communion with tradition, a getting back to the old ways. It is played across most of America west of the 100th meridian—from the plains of Canada to Oklahoma to California—by tribes as diverse as the Pawnee, the Blackfeet, Cheyenne and Crows (bitter enemies), the Piutes, Shoshonis, Miwocs, Modocs and Hupas, and under names ranging from hand game to stick game and from bone game to kill-the-bone, or *niaungpikai*.

It is an old, old game: gaming sticks and bone dice go back to 4000 B.C. at Danger Cave in Utah, a paradigm-primal-desert-

---

* In 1964, a team of biologists killed the oldest bristlecone of all on a mountainside in eastern California. They were drilling a test core to determine its age, when the drill broke. Rather than order another drill, they cut down the ancient tree with a chainsaw. It proved to be just under 5000 years old.

culture site. It is a live piece of the Neolithic. Up in Montana, where the Blackfeet, Paigan, Bloods and Flatheads play enormous games, there is a hundred-year-old hand-game master who is supposed to be a millionaire. When he plays, hundreds of people crowd around to make side bets at huge odds. He sits there, a skeleton, all in black, invisible behind dark glasses, a tall dark hat on his head. He cackles out his songs in an icy voice, and his opponents guess wrong ten, twenty, thirty times in a row; and when he guesses, he points with a long finger as unerring as death. When the game has ended—sometimes they go on for several days and nights—he drives away in a black Cadillac (they say), his pockets stuffed with money, titles to pickup trucks and papers to horses, deeds to alfalfa land and range. He twists the power of others against them: he is the blind samurai who cuts the flame off the candle, the singer of songs that trick, the foolmaker, the master.

The game that night outside of Bishop was between Bishop and the Piutes from Big Pine, the next town down the Owens Valley. The Bishop team had already beaten a team from the Modoc Reservation across the Sierra, and won the four-hundred-dollar first prize, plus a thousand or two in side bets. Not only Indians bet; white ranchers and cowboys also put their money in the pot. Like church bingo, the hand game is religious enough to be quasilegal, and it is far more exciting than the dead travesty of gambling most white men play: craps, blackjack, poker, roulette, the slot machine, the bookie—all fixed, the odds skewed till Jesus Christ himself couldn't win, not an ounce of magic to it. "Where are your songs?" a Piute gambler might ask his Anglo counterpart. "What gods, what spirits guide your aim?"

The basin version of the hand game goes something like this. Two teams of six or seven people face each other, kneeling on the ground about fifteen feet apart, a pile of bet money in the middle. Each team begins with a bundle of betting sticks. There are also two pairs of bones, hollow deer-bone cylinders about five inches long, each pair consisting of one striped and one plain.

The team that starts out holding the bones begins to chant a song, beating out a rhythm on logs in front of them, passing the bones back and forth. Then, as the chanting and the drumming grow louder, more intense, two members of the team each take a pair of bones and, hiding their hands behind their backs or behind a blanket or beneath a hat, they conceal the striped bone in one hand, the plain one in the other.

Then they hold out their fists—the chanting grows more defiant, warlike—and the other team tries to guess which hands hold which bones, striped or plain. If they guess both pairs of bones correctly, the bones go over to them. Then they begin to chant one of *their* game songs and conceal the bones for team number one to guess at. If they guess only one pair of bones correctly, the first team gets to hold the remaining bones and mix them up again for team number two to guess at. Right guesses win betting sticks; wrong ones lose them. When a team loses all of its sticks, the game is over and the bet money is divvied up between the winners and their backers. A single game can last anywhere from half an hour to all night and on into the next day, and a tournament may last a week. It is simple, the simplest of games; but there is a fierceness, a concentration to it, in the songs, the gestures, the pointing, that encompasses elements of *bushido,* high-stakes poker, grand opera. It is a war, fought with instincts, nerve, the third eye, if you will: What is one to make of a dozen right guesses in a row? There is a kind of skill going on here that I don't know.

The game that night was a pretty big one. There must have been a couple of thousand people watching, all but a few of them Indians. A bare bulb strung from the trees lit the playing ground. Inside the Indian Center building a rock dance was going on. Most of the crowd were drunk, getting drunk, hung over or some terrible combination of the three.

"Hey, Tom Watson. Hey, I'm gonna kick your ass, you old sonofabitch."

"Hey, Bill. Hey, you ain't gonna kick no ass long as I'm around. How you doin', anyway, you old sonofabitch?"

"I'm pretty good. I been workin' over on the Rogers Ranch,

over to Goldfield, last couple of months. What you been doin'?"

"I work for the county, drivin' a snowplow, las' winter"—for some mysterious reason, Piutes are naturally skillful heavy-equipment operators—"and I been *drunk* ever since!"

Only the very old still speak Piute or Shoshoni, whose dialects are so abstruse that a band from Bakersfield may not be able to communicate with a band from the Tehachapi Hills.

I talked to an old man in Can't-Bust-'Em overalls. "I played the hand game for twenty years down in Big Pine," he told me. "A bunch of us would just get together and play anytime—just to pass the time, you know. But I quit playing about twenty years ago. Oh, they just started drinking too much, and people would get drunk and get mad because they lost, and then there would be fights. It just wasn't fun anymore. When everybody started getting drunk and fighting, it just wasn't fun anymore." He shook his head with a kind of placid sorrow; there was something tortoiselike about this old man, a turtle's calm.

But he was right about the drinking. The hand-game grounds were littered with empty cans and bottles, and there was a constant stream of pickup trucks roaring off into the night on beer runs. People lugged cases of beer around or sneaked off to coolers hidden down by the river. You could almost get drunk on the yeasty air. A couple of thugs slugged it out at the edge of the crowd: roundhouse punches, most of them missing, the rest glancing, that looked like they could kill a man if they landed square. "Last year someone got knifed to death; the sheriff, he didn't like Indians, so he just let the guy bleed to death on the ground while he went around questioning people," someone told me; not angrily, just stating what to him was a cold fact. *Indian drinking*: whether it is due to oppression or acculturation or poverty or an enzyme missing in the Native American liver, it is an awful thing. "The water that banishes reason," one early alcoholic chief enthusiastically dubbed it. Tribes traded whole homelands for a keg of whiskey; drank away their holiest rituals, abandoned green prairies and ancient villages for honky-tonk towns and skid rows. It is an awful mystery, like cancer or madness.

But the game was a good one that night. The Bishop team looked formidable. There was a gigantic jolly-looking man who must have weighed three hundred solid pounds and who pulled frequently at a bottle of sweet peach brandy. There were two skinny, owlish old men in cowboy hats of straw, brothers perhaps, who looked like surprised Chinese. There were two young men, one with a black Stetson, the other a Mammoth Mountain ski-area T-shirt. And there were two young women next to them (sisters? wives?) with a striking, almost feral beauty. (A Piute girl from Bakersfield once told me, proudly, challenging, "No man can handle a Piute woman. They just can't. Sooner or later, we break loose and run wild. Never try and hold on to a Piute woman.")

The Big Pine team were all women. Was that band a matriarchy, as some Piute bands were supposed to be, I wondered? Old women, stout and hard as nails, rocking back and forth as they sang the old gambling songs that, a Piute friend told me later, summon up energy from pine nuts and foxes, crickets and mountains, crab lice and stars—wherever there is the tiniest glint of power, according to Piute metaphysics.

The Big Pine women were real tough, someone in the crowd told me. They had strong songs and sharp eyes, and they had won may games up and down the Owens Valley and beyond. But this night was definitely the Bishop team's night; there was a kind of thaumaturgy going on, and it was the Bishop men doing it. They sang from deep in the gut, as Tibetans do, as if voices were coming up out of the earth and resounding up their spines and out their mouths; and their songs were broken with shrill war cries and shouted insults. They drummed so hard that they whapped up dust from the logs, and they made arrogant, elegant gestures with sticks and hats in time to the music. When the Big Pine women guessed wrong, the Bishop players showed them the bones with mocking laughter, and the big, big man tipped back his bottle of brandy in an exaggerated victory toast, smacking his lips. You could not help but laugh, there was such joy in their winning; but the Big Pine women were not amused, and they threw their lost betting sticks at their opponents like little spears. The big man belly-laughed, "Ho ho ho!"

At times one of the players seemed to latch onto some extraordinary string of instinct and pulled himself along by it. Sometime long after midnight, the Bishop team lost one pair of bones; one of their young women held the second pair, and she meant to hold them. Her eyes shone with something like hunger, and she smiled as she sang with the rest of her team, the bones clenched in her fists, hard.

The Big Pine women guessed, guessed wrong, and she held the bones out to show them, laughter breaking her singing . . . The Bishop Indians went into another song, and she rubbed and shook the bones, whispered to them and palmed them again, and again the Big Pine women pointed with their sticks and pointed wrong. She held the bones out to them, laughing, teasing. "They're gonna whup 'em," a Bishop Indian next to me said, grinning.

And again the song rose, cutting as a hawk flies, dipping and soaring, rising and falling; and again she caressed the bones and made passes over them and then concealed them as she sang; and again they guessed wrong, and the crowd pushed in closer with a low roar of talk and laughter, sensing, smelling the power coming off her. "Yep, they're gonna whup 'em," the Indian next to me said again, grinning. And she held the bones again and again: seven more rounds, till finally someone pointed right, and the song died out . . . She laughed still and tossed the bones across to the Big Pine women carelessly, as if they had lost their significance. She had taken the fight out of them. A little more than a half-hour later, the game was over and the Bishop team and their backers were splitting up the bet money, a heap of crumpled bills, fives, tens and twenties. The Big Pine women walked away, muttering. I looked at the young girl who had held the bones: her face was still shining, and she stood among her laughing, talking companions in a kind of trance, smiling at nothing . . .

The gaming went on far, far into the night. After a while, the power loosed by the songs, and the unreality of ten right guesses or parries in a row, began to seem completely natural, even ordinary. We were standing among drunken magicians on the Indian side of a small American desert town, watching them try each other's magic. The treetops flexed in the night wind; you could smell the river and the grass.

When we left, the Bishop team was playing the boys from Owyhee, way up in Duck Valley, which is someplace beyond nowhere. Bishop held the bones, and they were singing and whipping out the beat with their sticks. There were whoops and bird cries: "*T'ku t'ku t'ku!*" The Owyhee men peered across the pile of money with bright, hard eyes. The next morning we heard that the Bishop team had beaten Owyhee and gone on to take the team from the Hee Hee Long House, way up in Oregon.

The Piutes say that most of their power comes from the earth. Any piece of earth will do, but some places, for some reason or another, are charged with a particular power, good, bad or just plain power, like electricity. There was a mountain tarn, for instance, where my friend from Bakersfield could not go. Every time she went there, she said, the Death Bird sang to her and then someone in her family died. "It used to be one of my favorite places," she said, "but I'll never go there again."

Some places are so powerful that they become shrines, places people go to learn or be healed or have a vision. These are not always the most obvious places. The tallest peak in a range, for instance, might be a place of no particular quality, while a mineral-streaked crag on a low-lying ridge may be the axis of spiritual energy for an entire valley system. Piute geography is different from ours. To us, land is dead, *real estate*: most of the Owens Valley, for instance, is somehow *owned* by the Los Angeles Department of Water and Power, which mines its ground water for irrigation and hydroelectric power to supply faraway LA. And shadowy men in that distant city have made great fortunes out of the snowmelt from the Sierra Nevada and the White Mountains, the little rain that falls on the Owens Valley and the ancient water deep in the aquifers. "How can someone *own* the rain?" a Piute might ask (you or I might ask the same question). It does sound crazy. One Indian I talked to assured me that the Europeans who populated the New World were all inhabitants of Bedlam, lunatics; and that the governments of Europe simply loaded them all on ships—to rid the Old World of them—and sent them over here. "And the white people are *still* all crazy," he said. I asked him if that included me, and he laughed and said, "You're not one of the *worst* cases."

But this land that Anglos think they own, even when they have never set foot on it or seen it, is covered with shrines— power places, if you will. Hanging out around Bishop and Big Pine that summer, and ranging as far as Topaz, the Panamints, the Tehachapi Hills, I began to hear about some of them. The place that seized my imagination the most was Mono Lake; I don't know why, but it was so. Mono wasn't that remote: it sat at the junction of two highways where the road over Tioga Pass to Yosemite cut off the main Las Vegas-Reno road; but for some reason, nobody seemed to go there or know anything about it. Even Owens Valley natives, such as Gordon, who had traversed the White Mountains in mid-winter and climbed all of the major peaks of the eastern Sierra, were vague about the place. People in Lee Vining, the little town at the western edge of the lake, knew little or less about it. It had seceded from the map somehow.

A Piute band lived around the lake until about 1920: some 250 of them, hunting the migratory birds that came there sea-sonally, seining brine shrimp from the saline waters, gathering the pupae of the brine flies that cluster at the water's edge and squeezing them into cakes for food. Some of these cakes were traded across the Sierra to the Yokuts Indians for acorns and furs. The Yokuts word for fly was *mono;* thus Mono Lake, the Lake of the Fly People.

Not much has ever happened there. Mark Twain explored the lake in the mid-nineteenth century and pronounced it "the loneliest spot on earth." A Frenchman named Cesare Cevirge (he must have been mad as a hatter, or wild as a wolf, or both) lived on Paoha, the largest of the lake's two islands, in the

1870s; he was a goatherd, he was unsuccessful and eventually he vanished.

In 1917 the McPherson family, who still live in the Mono area, moved onto the same island to homestead. They brought more goats and Belgian hares as big as bobcats, and raised crops on black volcanic soil irrigated by artesian wells. Old Wallis McPherson, who as a child lived on Paoha, told me of corn twelve feet high and eighteen-pound watermelons and shooting and roasting the phalaropes, the small, sweet birds that autumn on the lake. The McPhersons left the island in 1921, and since then the lake has been deserted.

What happened to the Mono Piutes? Captain John, the last chief of the tribe, died in 1930. He claimed to remember the Spanish priests coming through in 1820, looking for gold and souls, and Wallis McPherson remembers talking to him as a child—a thread of living history leading way, way back, to the Stone Age, medievalism and mercantilism. One day in 1930, Captain John decided his life had gone on long enough—he was 115, by his own reckoning. So, as the story goes, he said good-by to his friends and relatives, sat down in his woven willow chair and, a few days later, died.

Some of the Mono Piutes moved down to Bishop. One old woman who remembered the lake well said wistfully, "The lake was our life. All of the ducks and geese we ate when I was young came from the lake. We got rabbit fur, rabbit blankets, from around there—that's the only thing we slept in when we were babies. There is something so beautiful about such a place."

One evening, driving south out of Lee Vining, I picked up an old, crippled Indian, a raggedy man, one of the last of the Mono Piutes. I gave him a ride to the poor place he was living—a dilapidated trailer with no heat, no light, in a dry canyon southwest of the lake. There was a kind of encampment there: shacks, cabins, hutches, the broken-down carcasses of cars and trucks, and half-wild dogs running, wagging, yelping to greet the old man as he got out of the car. He was a kind-faced, resigned man. It was as if he had been through the very worst the world could throw at him, and now there was nothing left but the aching, wounded aftermath to live through. We drank whiskey by kerosene lamp in the chill of his trailer, and he told me how he had been crippled: "It happen' in the Korean War; I stepped on a mine. But it really happened way before that, when I was a young kid. I was walkin' through the hills way back there"—he gestured broadly across the mountains—"and I turned over a rock and found this perfect crystal knife. Like a fool, I took it, thinking it was worth something. Then one day I showed it to an old man who knew about things, and he said, 'Charlie, take it back and put it back where you found it. The Old People left those stones there, and if you move one, something bad will happen.' So I took it back and left it there, right where I found it." He laughed, a soft laugh. "It was a beautiful knife. You never seen anything like it. It was like a *diamond.*" His voice was distant, as if retelling a dream. "But I never should have taken it. Two years later, in the war, I got my legs half blown off. Ever since then, things have been pretty tough." I didn't know what to say; it seemed as if the Fly People had had a hard end.

That October I got together a wooden canoe and a sackful of gear and headed out onto the lake.

If there were a lake on the moon, it would look like Mono: the Sea of Sighs, with the dust turned to water. The shores are bleached, mineral. To the south, gray volcanic cones and rivers of hard slag. Tarnished hills to the north. To the east, the absolute being and nothingness of Nevada. A harsh, uncompromising place. October was a good time to come: it was cool, but not icy, and the great flocks of eared grebes were migrating through, on their way south to wintering grounds on the Pacific coast of the United States and Mexico. Three quarters of a million of them—a Jerusalem, a Los Angeles of birds.

I set out in the crystalline light of dawn, lugging canoe and pack down the gravel beaches of the western shore and then mucking through the brittle, exposed alkali flats at water's edge. Deer had stamped a web of trails from sagebrush, where they grazed, to freshwater springs and back; and there were coyote prints crossing here and there. A big buck jackrabbit leapt stupidly from the brush, goggled at me, then lolloped away. If I had been a coyote or an old-time Piute with a throwing stick, he would have been dead. The sun had not yet risen: the old lake was like a bronze mirror corroded green.

I paddled out onto the lake, and all at once I was among thousands and thousands of birds—grebes, taut, drab little birds with anxious eyes. They drifted imperceptibly away as my canoe approached. So many of them! Three quarters of a million is only a number until it is catalyzed into life. The air was filled with the rustling of billions of feathers, a white sound, like wind or distant water. Looking down where my oar cut, I could see the lake water boiling with brine shrimp; cup up a handful of lake water and there were perhaps a score of them, feathery, transulent things. The lake was a living broth. Everywhere, almost to the limits of vision, birds swam and dove and fed: the dance of life and death, of algae and diatoms, of shrimp and flies and birds, in the sepulchral heart of that stony country, of all places.

During that first, lone trip I spent several days on the lake's two islands: Negit, an ebony volcanic cone; and Paoha, the eerie blanched little continent of pale, wasted hills. The two islands were opposite as yin and yang. Indeed, the Piutes think that the islands are the bodies of the gods of good and evil, who fought in the sky over the lake, slew each other and fell dead into the water—or so some people say. There are a lot of bastard "Indian" legends in the West that hold more whiskey than water.

Negit means island of the blue-winged gull in Piute—a typical straightforward aboriginal place-name. In the summer Negit is a rookery for some 50,000 California gulls who flock here from the Pacific, from the beaches around Los Angeles, to breed. By the time they leave, their numbers have swollen to over 80,000. In gull season the sky is full of their discordant music, and the stones are basted with limey excrement.

But in October the island was deserted. I landed on a silent shore littered with feathers and with airy bird skeletons frozen in alkali that looked like they might take to the air in an instant. I labored up the steep slopes of the old volcano, where sagebrush glowed; and on the summit a monarch butterfly drifted out of the crater, a tiny eruption of gold. I looked down on cinder slopes, onto white alkaline shores and the green sea and the sierra wall with its first dusting of autumn snow beyond. There were more birds in the lake than water, it seemed: shoals, fields of them, clotted almost solid here and there where they crowded together to feed on concentrations of brine shrimp.

There are three great bird migrations, and many small ones, that pass through Mono. The three great ones are the gulls, the grebes and, in the late summer, the phalaropes. These last are the most remarkable, not for their numbers, but for the length of their annual journeys. A hundred thousand Wilson's phalaropes fly through on their way from the northern Great Basin to wintering grounds in Argentina. But even more remarkable are the 20,000 or so northern phalaropes who drift through on their way from their breeding grounds in the subarctic tundra of the Old and New worlds to winter off the west coast of South America, in the Humboldt Current. One of these tiny birds—an adult weighs scarcely an ounce and a half—could fit easily in your cupped hands; and yet they cover half the planet in their peregrinations and somehow, year after year, find this salt lake in the corner of the Great Basin. Is there a tiny astrolabe scrawled deep on each chromosome; some intricate glyph of land form, curve of river, crumple of mountain, writ in the blood? It is a marvel.

That afternoon I rowed across to the white island, rippling the meadows of birds with my passing. *Paoha,* the white island's Piute name, means island of the spirits with the waving hair, because of its fumaroles, or the alkali storms that whirl off its colorless bluffs. There was something vaguely sinister about the place, and I didn't explore much (afraid, perhaps, of what I might find on the island or within myself). Perversely, it was Halloween and the moon was full: food for nightmares when you are alone.

The McPherson farm still stood on a headland at the south-western end of the island, its abandoned buildings somehow making the desolation seem more desolate. The irrigation system had long since broken down, and the place was dry, all alkali dunes, diatomaceous hills and dry brush that crackled like parchment. It was like a little scrap of the Gobi cast adrift in a saline sea. It would be hard to imagine a more barren place without looking at photographs of the surface of the moon or the screes of Mars. Most of the goats and the hares were dead: I found their corpses mummified in the chemical dust, leather ghosts.

Still, there was a presence of some kind. The island wasn't ugly or awful; it was merely *extreme*. It was not a place meant for men to live; perhaps that was its special charm. It was on another wave length completely, one that had nothing to do with me or my dreams of adventure or my search for secrets. There was nothing there for me.

One evening, walking the lunar hills that rib the island, I spooked a great horned owl from the dead black willow tree by the old McPherson barn. A giant of a bird, he might have been a man dressed up as an owl. He glared at me with chill yellow eyes for a long minute, flew away to the east, crossing a mile of sky with three mighty flexings of his wings, and was gone, leaving an indecipherable message in my mind. Paoha disturbed me, in some way I cannot put my finger on. I dreamt all night, every night, there—daft dreams and dreams within dreams, the kind you wake up from only to find yourself in the middle of another one. I would rise in the morning exhausted, drained, as if vampires had been at me in the night. It was only by putting my attention to everyday things—rubbing oil in my shoes (the alkali can crack a pair of leather shoes to pieces in a day), gathering firewood, keeping my journal, watching the birds—that I did not go a long way round the bend.

The great lakes of the basin that I know—Mono, Pyramid, Winnemucca, Mud, Owens—are all dead or dying; and I suppose that the birds that depend on them in their yearly sun-ruled dances must die also.

Mono, for instance. In 1940 the Los Angeles Department of

Water and Power began taking water from the Mono Basin. All but one of the lake's five major arteries—Rush, Lee Vining, Parker and Walker creeks—were diverted, and their waters exported to LA. In 1970, with the opening of the second Los Angeles aqueduct, water exports from the Mono Basin were increased. Since 1940 the lake has fallen some 40 vertical feet, and it is currently falling at a rate of about 1.6 feet a year. In the last three years Negit Island has become a peninsula, its gull rookery open to predation from coyotes, bobcats, wild dogs, men. As its fresh-water dilution decreases, the lake grows more alkaline: it now has a PH factor of about 9.7, approximately that of caustic lye. It scalds the skin. No one is certain what this chemical concentration will do to the shrimp and the brine flies and the birds that feed on them.

A hundred miles to the south, there was once a lake named Owens that was, like Mono, an inland sea. Steamships crossed it during the mining era, hauling supplies to the mining camps in the Inyo Mountains. Today, its waters diverted to feed southern California's feverish coast, Owens is a grim mix of dust bowl, chemical pan and lye marsh. In wet years enough melt water leaks down into the old lake bed to give it a pitiful temporary rebirth: for a month or so, the lake shines in its primordial way. Then the earth swallows the water up, the sun sucks it dry and the lake reverts to ghosthood. This could well be Mono's fate within a century, some naturalists say—to survive only as a myth, a spectral presence, a hole in the country where something was and still should be, but is not.

Pyramid Lake, north of Reno, is another of the dying dead seas of the basin country. Captain John Fremont was the first white man to see it, on January 16, 1844, traveling south from The Dalles, Oregon, searching for a nonexistent river that was supposed to run south out of the basin. He came down through the dreadful country of Malheur, the Black Rock and Smoke Creek deserts, dragging a howitzer with him in case he ran into any Spanish. He wrote in his journal:

Leaving a signal for the party to encamp, we continued our way up the hollow, intending to see what lay beyond the mountain. The hollow was several miles long, forming a good pass; the snow deepening to about a foot as we neared the summit. Beyond, a defile between the mountains descended rapidly about two thousand feet; and, filling up all the lower space, was a sheet of green water, some twenty miles broad. It broke upon our eyes like the ocean. The neighboring peaks rose high above us, and we ascended one of them to obtain a better view. The waves were curling in the breeze, and their dark-green color showed it to be a body of deep water. For a long time we sat enjoying the view, for we had become fatigued with mountains, and the free expanse of moving waves was very grateful. It was set like a gem in the mountains.

My only quarrel with Fremont is his eye for color: the waters of Pyramid Lake are like nothing I have ever seen. The closest I can come to describing them is "neon turquoise," "infrablue," "indigo fire"; all I am really revealing is the poverty of language when set against landscape. But it is surely no mere "dark-green."

I first came to Pyramid Lake from the south. Again, I was following a cold trail of rumor and campfire gossip. The summer before, a climber in Yosemite Valley, drunk as only climbers can be, told me a long, rambling series of stories about the lake—stories you had to believe because they were so unreasonable. Wovokah, the ghost-dance prophet, the Piute who dreamt up the whole ghost-dance religion, had traveled all the way from his Utah homeland to Pyramid Lake to die; he was buried on the shores of the lake, but the local Piutes would not say where. Like Crazy Horse, he vanished at death, to rise again someday . . .

In the Terraced Hills north of the lake were caves jull of mummies, mummies wrapped in gold leaf. (Someone told someone, who told someone else; like all such caves, they were lost, of course.) There had once been a tribe—called the Lovelock People by archeologists—who lived around the lake. They wore pelican-skin cloaks and woven-basket hats and deerskin boots. Sometime, perhaps as recently as a hundred years ago, they vanished; nobody knows why or where . . .

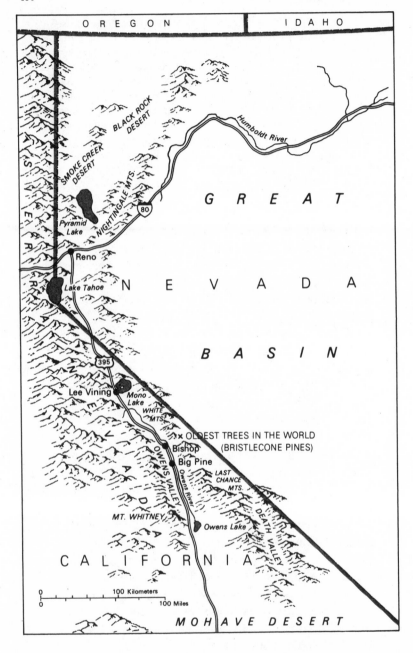

There was supposed to be an underground river between Pyramid and Walker Lake, which is a good hundred miles to the south. A few years back, a man drowned in Pyramid Lake and his body turned up in Walker two weeks later—a tall, tall tale.

On a more solid level, there was a kind of fish in Pyramid, a primitive bottom-feeder called a cui-ui (pronounced "kwee-wee"), a kind of living fossil. The Pyramid Lake Piutes used to net them where the Truckee River feeds into the lake, and smoke them. They were an important food source, weighing up to ten pounds each; a stable, protein-rich food, they made the Pyramid people aristrocrats among the local Digger tribes. Well, according to some authorities, the cui-ui *(Chasmistes cujus)* are found in only two places on earth: in Pyramid Lake and in a lake in the interior deserts of Asia, on the other side of the world. Both lakes are landlocked. Now, there's a biological riddle to chew on.

I spent a week around Pyramid Lake and came away none the wiser. The Indians would tell me nothing—nothing I wanted to know, at any rate. The country around the lake was too dreadful to explore in summer's heat: Hardscrabble Creek (dry), Winnemucca Lake (dry); Jigger Bob, Hell's Kitchen and Poison canyons. Most of the 8,000 white pelicans who nest on Anoha Island at the south end of the lake were gone, flown south to Central America for the autumn. I found one dead off in the sagebrush, shot by some fool. The wingspan must have been a good six feet, and each wing was light as air, as long as my arm and probably ten times as strong. The feathers were black, gray and brightly white as snow. Even in death, there was a balletic grace to the bird.

But the place itself eluded me. The water was hard to drink: it was warm and tasted almost exactly like two teaspoons of borax dissolved in a glass of tap water. The dry mountains roundabout blazed like hell. When I took my kayak out one evening, a sudden squall almost swamped me. It was as if the place wanted to be left alone.

Pyramid Lake is dying. In 1905 whites began to cut off the

waters of the Truckee River before they reached the lake, and now Pyramid falls about 1.2 vertical feet a year—80 vertical feet so far. As you drive in from the south, you pass through Anglo farmlands, wet and green; when the land turns brown, you know you have reached Indian country.

The Pyramid Lake tribe was involved in a water-rights struggle with Anglo landholders upstream on the Truckee, but the tribal chairman, a broad, brown man wearing a Coors beer hat and bearing the unlikely name of Vidovich, seemed strangely unconcerned. When I asked him about the value of the lake to his people—there were once some 5,000 of them living around the lake; today there are less than 900, three quarters of them unemployed—he shrugged, laughed and said, "Why bother? We could get rich off the lake, but we like it just the way it is. Why mess with it?" It was a perfect answer for a Buddha, or an innocent; and no one has ever been able to tell the two apart, as far as I know.

The Basin lakes go back about 70,000 years, when water from the melting Ice Age glaciers filled up hollows and furrows in the basin floor. Much of eastern Nevada was an ocean—the Lahontan Sea. Pyramid and Walker lakes are the last, perishing remnants of it. Mono and Owens lakes were also inland seas, pockets of Pleistocene melt water. Mud and Winnemucca lakes are already gone; the others, it seems, will soon follow. There is nothing more one can say about it: there is nothing emptier, more gloriously useless, than a value judgment. I happen to think that great white pelicans (a single one!) are more important than the tiny, scrabbling schemes of land speculators and their kept politicians in southern California. Still, who the hell am I? About 219 million Americans would probably say I am wrong.

It is a moot point, anyway: what will endure, will endure; what will die, will die. Everything will die, given enough time.

"Desert" is relative; deserts may be austere or harsh, but most deserts are violently alive. Desert plants fairly *incandesce* with life; desert animals are lean, sly, full of a rage to survive. When you find a dead desert, you can bet, nine times out of ten, that man was there to kill it.

The Owens Valley, for instance: there were farms and orchards up and down the valley—the desert bloomed—before Los Angeles sucked the water away. Take Manzanar, site of the internment camp for Japanese-Americans during World War II. The name actually means "apple orchards"; today Manzanar is a dusty little Gobi of a place, a scorpion ranch. Between Bishop and Independence, you see dozens of abandoned farms and homesteads, orchards of deadwood.

During the summer of the great drought a few years back, when the whole West was drying up from the Great Plains to the Pacific, I passed through LA. You never would have known there was a drought. In San Francisco water was rationed but in Los Angeles the swimming pools were operating, sprinklers spewed water over the golf courses and freeway greenbelts; 95 percent of the sewage LA loosed into the ocean was fresh water, unrecycled. Meanwhile, Mono Lake was falling; the few remaining ranches and farms left in the Owens Valley were cooking away in the sun.

For some spirited Owens Valley patriot, it was just too much: a mysterious dynamite blast destroyed the California Aqueduct down in the southern part of the valley. Water spilled into the dry bed of Owens Lake, reviving the hibernating shrimp and pupfish populations; flocks of gulls flew all the way from the Pacific to feed. For a few days until the crews from LA could repair the shattered pipeline, it was almost like the good old days: the desert was flowered with fishes, birds and the blessed green voices of water. The FBI was sent in to track down the saboteur, but found little help from the valley people. A mountain-climber friend was having coffee at Lee Vining, or maybe it was Tom's Place, or Lone Pine—one of those lonesome little eastern California towns—when a local highway patrolman, a friend of his, came in. They got to talking about the blowing up of the aqueduct. "That sure was a shame," the cop said with ponderous sarcasm. "Yep, a real crime. And I'll bet those two FBI men they have working in the garage in Bishop, the ones pretendin' to be mechanics, won't ever find out who did it, either."

The last time I was out in the eastern California desert, some of the Piutes I met were talking about something called the Piute Warrior Society. They had cached rusty old automatic weapons somewhere and black-market dynamite; they talked of uniting all of the frail little bands of Shoshonis and Piutes in the western Great Basin and occupying some of their lost native lands: enough to hunt and gather on again, the traditional way. There would be no pickup trucks, no whiskey, no television, not even a Stetson or a pair of cowboy boots.

I didn't say anything—why argue with a dream?—but it sounded to me like the ghost dance all over again. Wovokah, the ghost-dance prophet, was right: if you danced long enough, the white man—the *inilladui,* the tramp, the rootless one— would wither away, as all rootless things do. But you had to dance a long, long time: these things take time.

Like all millennialists, the Piute warriors were impatient: they wanted salvation within a lifetime. But they should just wait; we won't be around that long.

Los Angeles is a chimerical thing, a Catherine wheel of a city; Las Vegas is a hallucination; Reno is like one of those little crystal gardens that children grow, which disintegrate when you tap them with a fingernail. Anglo life in the Great Basin is a transitory thing, based on ever-diminishing returns; deep down, we are poor, poor people, poorer than the poorest Digger who ever cracked a cricket between his teeth.

I went to college with the Piute girl who grew up in Bakersfield; her father worked as a construction foreman, and her mother, who passed as a Chicana, went to mass every night. They lived in the suburbs. This girl graduated from college and went on to take a master's degree in sociology. Today she takes peyotl and is learning to speak Piute from her grandmother; her hair has grown out, long and wild and tied with feathers, and she wanders through the Poverty Hills by herself, looking for the secret springs, dwarf forests, illuminated chasms. Things come full circle, given time.

Long after we have gone (God knows where) and abandoned the back country, there will stand, by a still lake that looks as if it was snipped out of tin, one of those lovely houses woven from wands, the kind they don't make anymore. And inside they will be passing the bones and pointing with their sticks, faces dark as old blood. I saw it, in a dream.

Los Angeles, and Other Lost Cities

THE ROAD TO LOS ANGELES, THE TRUE ROAD, BEGINS AT A Navaho trading post called Nageezi, forty-nine miles southeast of Farmington, New Mexico. Driving west from Nageezi, you find yourself crossing a desolate land, hills, gullies, Navaho sheep camps here and there, shacks and debris of junked cars. The country is—not beautiful.

This is the checkerboard area of the Navaho reservation, so called because every other square mile is owned by the Navahos, every other by the railroads and big mining and energy companies. This land-ownership pattern goes back to 1862, when Lincoln signed the Homestead Act. Not only did the Homestead Act open up the West for small farmers, it also granted 20 million acres of public domain to big business. As the railroads moved West, the government turned over even more land to them, including hundreds of square miles in checkerboard patterns along railroad rights of way.

The checkerboard land southwest of Nageezi is not pretty, but it is valuable: beneath it geologists have discovered a bed of coal thirty feet thick in places and as wide as Rhode Island; also pockets of gas and oil, with seams of uranium ore here and there.

The Indians who live out here—the Navahos of Burnham, Newcomb, Naschitti and other dirt-poor hamlets—are not happy about living on top of all this fossil fuel and radioactive bullion. First of all, all they really want to do is herd sheep, and you can't herd sheep in the middle of a strip mine. Large-scale mining in the desert puts an end to farming and grazing forever, destroying the range and sucking the aquifers so dry that they don't recover for generations. Second, the Navahos of the checkerboard area are realists. They have already seen the future in the Four Corners Power Plant just to the north and west of Farmington. The Four Corners Power Plant burns

Navaho coal and sells the electricity to Los Angeles; the energy companies get rich, LA gets power and the Navahos get two tons of fly ash a day spewed into their air. Breathing west of the plant in the direction of the prevailing winds is like sucking on an exhaust pipe.

Thirty miles out of Nageezi, you cross Escavada Wash and descend into Chaco Canyon. Back around 1000 A.D., Chaco Canyon was the Los Angeles of the Colorado Plateau. The canyon floor was a patchwork of fields and a series of tiny city-states—Pueblo Bonito, Chetro Ketl, Hungo Pavi, Casa Chiquita, Wijiji, Penasco Blanco, Casa Rinconada, Kin Kletso, Tsin Kletzin, Una Vida, Pueblo del Arroyo—strung along the canyon and its rims. Pueblo Bonito ("Beautiful Little City," the old Spanish named it) is the most impressive of the ruins. It is a jewel of a town. A single half-moon–shaped building, its 200-yard-long flat side facing south, Pueblo Bonito contains more than 600 rooms and 33 kivas; it is 5 stories high at its tallest point.

As I said, Pueblo Bonito is a jewel. Its stone walls, built of delicately intersticed slabs of dense, hard sandstone, are up to three feet thick: they will be standing when Albuquerque and LA are in ruins. The more archeologists study the place, the more remarkable it becomes. Its internal workings are as delicate as a Swiss watch: in fact, the town was actually designed as a giant timepiece. Certain windows are angled so that on solstices, beams of sunlight filter through to strike an inner wall. A few miles from Pueblo Bonito, at the edge of Chaco Canyon, is a rock tower called Fajada Butte. A few years ago an archeologist stumbled on an Anasazi ritual calendar at the base of the butte. A series of rock slabs were arranged before a spiral carved in the face of the cliff. Precisely at noon on the summer solstice, the sun shone between the slabs, casting a thin line of blazing light across the center of the spiral, bisecting it vertically. The Sun Dagger, it has been named.

At its peak Pueblo Bonito had a population of about 1,000; the whole canyon held perhaps 5,000 or 6,000 people in its dozen-odd towns. Sometime around 1300 A.D., they moved away. No one is sure why—drought, exhaustion, loss of will, erosion, as too many trees were felled for too many house beams.

The canyons and deserts of the Southwest are full of dead cities: Grand Gulch, Mesa Verde, the perfect, intricate cliff rookeries of Betatakin and Keet Seel in far-off Tsegi Canyon; Hovenweep, Chaco, Inscription House . . . The people moved on and settled along the Rio Grande on the Hopi mesas and at Zuñi, where they live today. Desert cities don't last forever— even the cleverest and loveliest of them, like Pueblo Bonito, have not survived. Look at Mohenjodaro in Pakistan; Casa Grande in the Chihuahuan Desert; Jiaohe in west China, along the old Silk Road—all great desert cities; all deserted, dead.

To understand Los Angeles, you have to start at a place like Pueblo Bonito. Los Angeles, too, is a desert city. It may be bigger, grander, than Pueblo Bonito, but that in itself is no guarantee that it will last longer. The best a desert city can do is, like Pueblo Bonito, to leave a lovely set of ruins, walls and rooms of a certain grace, colors smoldering on broken pottery, figurines of forgotten gods still charged with a tenuous power . . .

The first Los Angeles was a Gabrielino Indian village called Yang-na. It was a village of tule-reed huts that looked like giant beehives, and it was located near what is now downtown LA. There were some twenty-eight Gabrielino villages in the basin of the Los Angeles, San Gabriel and Santa Ana rivers. When Juan Rodriguez Cabrillo, a Portuguese captain employed by the Spanish, sailed into San Pedro Bay in 1542, he saw smoke rising from these villages and he named the place Bahia de los Fumos, a prescient name and classic inadvertent joke. Yang-na and the other Gabrielino villages are, of course, long gone, buried deep beneath the Ventura Freeway, the Strip, Danny's Terriyaki Okie-Dog.

According to historians, the last Gabrielino died around 1910; but long before that, their way of life had been almost totally extinguished. The first meeting between the Spanish and the "kumi.vit," as the Gabrielinos called themselves, was in 1769. "We gave them a little tobacco and some glass beads, and they went away pleased," Father Crespi, the obligatory Spanish priest, wrote. By 1771 a mission had been established at San Gabriel, and by the 1780s the kumi.vit had effectively lost their independence and were well on their way to becoming the subproletariat of the pueblo of Los Angeles. The Gabrielinos and remnants of neighboring tribes, such as the Serrano, the Luiseno, the Cahuilla and the Ipai-Ipai, became anonymous serfs.

Little is known of the Gabrielinos, but that little bit is intriguing. The women tattooed themselves from their eyes down to their breasts; they wore flowers in their long hair and gowns made from dozens of bird skins sewn together—lucifer hummingbirds, vermilion flycatchers, goldfinches, coppery flickers—the feathers shimmering madly as they walked.

I have a photograph of a kumi.vit sandstone mortar and pestle. The shapes are so finely wrought—the hip of a wave, the knee of a cloud, completely unforced curves, easy angles—that it is hard to comprehend that these were tools used in everyday tasks. They are so airily graceful that you feel you could sail those same shapes halfway to the moon with a flick of a wrist. Somehow, that ultimate mortar and pestle, and the idea of those gorgeous gowns smelling faintly of old dried bird's blood, tell me that the Gabrielino were a people with a deep, abiding sense of how things should be. There was a righteousness— what the Chinese call *jen*, the Buddhists *dharma*—in their very household tools. Anthropologists also tell us that the Gabrielino spoke an Uto-Aztecan language, that they smoked pipes inlaid with abalone-shell mosaic, and that their major deity was Qa-o-ar, a name so sacred that it was only whispered during ceremonies. (As this last piece of information comes to us through the Spanish friars, I like to think that "Qa-o-ar" is really a kumi.vit obscenity passed on by some Indian jokester.)

To the Spanish, of course—the same Spanish who smashed and melted down the fantastic gods and masks, statues and ornaments of the Incas into gold and silver bullion, and then lost most of that same dead weight of bullion when their worm-cankered fleets foundered on their way home to the Old World—the people they called Gabrielinos (after the archangel Gabriel) were so much cheap, expendable labor for their empire. By 1785 the Indians were officially made a separate laboring peasant class. In 1835 the Mexican government began to secularize and seize church property, and in retaliation the padres slaughtered cattle, cut down orchards and burned crops. The Indians, whose labors had built up the mission system, lost everything. From 1860 to 1900 smallpox epidemics decimated the surviving kumi.vit.

But the story has a strange footnote. In 1973 a group of Indian-looking people surfaced in San Gabriel; they were, they claimed, the last of the kumi.vit, heirs to the spiritual mortgage of Los Angeles. They hadn't died out at all. They had been there all along, only nobody had noticed.

More irony: the first time I came to Los Angeles, it was to meet an Indian. Los Angeles is the great Indian city of modern North America. More Navahos live there than in Gallup, New Mexico; more Sioux than in Rapid City, South Dakota. There are Eskimos, and Yaquis from Mexico. LA Indian culture is unique, a blend of tribal traditions, pan-Indian syncretisms and the weird culture of Los Angeles itself. Medicine men with faces brown and wrinkled as tobacco leaves have built sweat lodges in backyards in unlikely places like Ventura and Pomona; drums throb in the suburban night; shamans wear shiny suits, live in railroad hotels and carry their eagle feathers, leathery dried turtle hearts and Thunder Flints in battered pawnshop suitcases. They can make it rain in an East LA barroom on Saturday night. Native American car clubs prowl the strip in electric-blue low-rider cars with zebra-striped plush upholstery.

The woman I had come to LA to see was named Hashi Hanta. A photographer friend named Max, the same Max I hiked the Barranca del Cobre with, had gotten to know her through the American Indian movement and decided I should meet her.

Hashi Hanta was a Choctaw Indian, born thirty-five years ago in Orange County. There is a photograph in the Bureau of Ethnography files at the Smithsonian Institute in Washington, D.C., taken in 1909 at Bayou Lacombe, Louisiana. It shows a Choctaw man, a Neolithic man, aiming a blowgun skyward. That past was long, long gone. Most of the Choctaws, along with the other of the so-called Five Civilized Tribes, were deported from the southeast in 1832, orders of President Andrew Jackson. A third of the Choctaw Nation died on the way west to Oklahoma; the survivors lived on a reservation in southeastern Oklahoma for a while, and then that, too, was taken away from them, the land turned over to white farmers and land speculators. A few thousand Choctaws live in Oklahoma today; a few hundred survive on a reservation near Philadelphia, Mississippi. One of Hashi Hanta's brothers is a filmmaker in Boston; another teaches on the reservation in Mississippi (teaching Choctaw language to the young, English to the old); a third is in a federal penitentiary somewhere— exile, the great, overwhelming fact of twentieth-century life.

We sat in Max's apartment in the Hollywood Hills, looking down on the night lights of Los Angeles. The apartment was bare except for a mattress on the floor: Max had just returned from a long series of magazine assignments on the road to find that his landlady had evicted him. His possessions were stacked out in the driveway, and he had two days to find a new place to live. She had even taken the light bulbs. We sat on the floor in the dim, empty room, American refugees. Hashi Hanta talked; she was a tiny, pretty woman, and laughter leaked out around her angry words like quicksilver squirting from a clenched fist.

She worked as a radio news broadcaster, writer and a waitress, she said. She owned an old house in East LA, with an unruly garden out back. She drove an enormous old sedan she called her pow-wow car. She had a teen-aged son she referred to as the disco Indian because all he liked to do was party and dance.

"I wish I had a few acres of land off somewhere in the country," she said wistfully. "That's how I would like to live. But at the same time you have an obligation to leave the world a better place than you found it. I would love to go out and live on the land, live the old ways. But there's no place to hide. I don't enjoy fighting; I don't enjoy the FBI chasing me around"—at that time, she was heavily involved in the radical side of LA Native American politics—"it's a horrible way to live; but you have no choice. Somehow I manage to survive." And then she said something that, looking back on it, was the soul of Choctaw LA: "You know, what I'd really like to do is to go to Tijuana and study and become the greatest lady bull-fighter in the world!"

Somehow the Indians of Los Angeles seem like an omen to me: 50,000 Ishmaels saying, by their very presence, "As you are, I was; as I am, you shall be."

LA is full of omens, and none of them are very good. Hill-topping, for instance: to make more room for housing develop-ments, whole hills in the Hollywood and Beverly ranges have been scalped and the excess earth dumped into gullies as landfill; $500,000 houses are then built on this manmade geol-ogy. These artificial environments are extremely fragile. Dur-ing the winter rains, whole streets of expensive suburbs slide to destruction. And if the rains don't get you, the fires will. During the dry season, the scorching Santa Ana winds whip through the coastal hills; dry as tinder, the scrub-oak chapparal goes up in apocalyptic brushfires, taking whole outlying neighborhoods with it. Scarved in flames, its foundations gnawed away by the rain, its lower levels awash in its own effluvial smoke, the whole imperious majesty of the city balances on the San An-dreas fault line like a drunk on a slack wire.

But water is the real question regarding LA. In her book *The White Album*, Joan Didion has a fascinating essay on *where the water comes from* in Los Angeles. "The water I will draw tomorrow from my tap in Malibu is today crossing the Mojave Desert from the Colorado River," Didion writes; and she describes the intricate computer-directed workings of California's water system, in which water from the Sacramento Delta, the eastern Sierra, the Colorado River and so on is shuffled around to irrigate great mechanized farms, industrial plants and cities.

From Didion, go on to George Sibley. Sibley, a stern, iconoclastic Colorado writer, wrote a piece in the October 1977 *Harper's* that should be required reading for all greater Los Angeles residents. In his article "The Desert Empire," Sibley points out that when the Colorado River was "divided up" in 1921 between southern California, Colorado, Arizona, Mexico and the rest, the river averaged just under 17 million acre-feet a year. To be on the safe side, the river czars figured on 15 million acre-feet annually, but from 1929 to 1969 there was a dry cycle, and the Colorado averaged only 13.1 million acre-feet yearly. Total use of Colorado River water today stands at 12.1 million acre-feet a year, which happens to be the river's total annual flow, without a drop left over. In two or three decades, Sibley projects, total use of Colorado River water will reach 15 million acre-feet a year. "This means," Sibley concludes, "that either we had better head into a wet cycle damn soon, or we will be approaching the day when there is nothing left in Lakes Powell and Mead but a gurgle." Eighty percent of southern California's water comes from the Colorado River.

Angelenos are arrogant; like the Cairenes or Luxorites of pharaonic Egypt, like Nebuchadnezzar's Babylonians, they see their city as the center of the world. It is El Dorado, Cibola, Jerusalem, Mecca, Lhasa, where gods and glamour are made. It is where the Maltese falcon roosts. Shelley's "Ozymandias" would have made a good Angeleno:

> "My name is Ozymandias, king of kings:
> Look on my works, ye Mighty, and despair!"
> Nothing beside remains. Round the decay
> Of that colossal wreck, boundless and bare,
> The lone and level sands stretch far away.

William Mulholland was the Ozymandias of LA, actually. It was Mulholland who began the hydrological imperialism that greater Los Angeles grew great on: the annexation of the San Fernando Valley in 1913, the almost military seizure of the Owens Valley water and the importation of lower Colorado River water through the Coachella Canal and the Colorado River Aqueduct. That same night in the summer of 1977, while mystical commandos were blowing up the Los Angeles Aqueduct in the Owens Valley, someone fired an arrow with a blasting cap attached to the tip into the chest of the statue of William Mulholland in front of the headquarters building of the Los Angeles Department of Water and Power.

Say it is 1990 and the Rockies slide into a dry winter. The high peaks are still not covered with snow by January 1, 1991. Wet spring snows come in March and April, but the snow pack in the mountains is still only a third or a quarter of the average when the spring runoff begins. A couple of small ski areas go bankrupt that winter, but in southern California no one notices the dry winter much: there is three years' worth of water stored up in the elaborate system of dams on the Colorado, and Los Angeles and the surrounding farmlands still get their annual fix. In the meantime, there is still LA's share of the annual 4 million acre-feet delivered by the California Aqueduct, as well as the other aqueducts, pipes and ditches of the California State Water Project.

In the winter of 1991–92, the Rockies are again hit by drought; and this time, the Sierras get it too. Despite the new dam on the Dolores River, the bean fields up around Dove Creek and Cortez are drying up and blowing away: there just isn't enough water. Down in the checkerboard area of the Navaho Reservation, the range begins to die: the aquifers are being sucked dry by strip mining. It is harder and harder for the energy companies to pump water for their slurry lines and the other arcane systems that mine coal and convert it into electricity—electricity, incidentally, that LA runs on.

Two years later they are talking about a great drought in the

West, the kind that ran the Anasazis out of Tsegi Canyon, Mesa Verde and the other ghost cities of the Southwest eight hundred-odd years ago. The oil-shale industry of northwestern Colorado, heavily dependent on ground and riverine water, has been forced to slow to a stumble. Denver, which gets much of its water from the headwaters of the Colorado piped through the Rockies in tunnels, is suing for a bigger share of the upper Colorado's flow. The grand canals of the Central Arizona Project, which were to supply a million acre-feet a year to the Phoenix-Tucson megalopolis, are almost dry. There isn't a lawn alive from Santa Monica to Omaha.

Two years later the United States arbitrarily cuts off Mexico's 1.5 million acre-foot share of the lower Colorado. Ranching and farming on the Great Plains west of the 100th meridian are dead: the aquifers and the Rocky Mountain-fed rivers, such as the Platte and the Arkansas, are not sufficient to support them. California is suing itself to death over allocation of the remnant waters of the CWP; every week in the summer of '96, the Los Angeles Aqueduct is sabotaged by Owens Valley commandos. LA and Las Vegas are vast brownouts; at night, they look like costume jewelry dipped in dust . . .

How many people lived in America west of the 100th meridian before the white man came? Two million? Three? Was there a good reason for this?

The coyotes must know something. They are moving back into the edges of Los Angeles, into places like Bel Air, Topanga, Lancaster, Tarzana. Every month or so there is a coyote story in the papers: a coyote pack was sighted running down a suburban street at two in the morning; recently, a woman looked out in her backyard and saw a strange gray shadow, a shadow that turned into a coyote, seized her pet poodle in its jaws, leapt over the fence and vanished. They live in the chaparral canyons and, some people say, under the freeways, in the culverts and storm drains . . .

Coyotes in the streets, medicine men in the skid-row hotels: What do they know that we don't know? Do they smell a drought in the wind? Hear the dry snicker of dunes drifting over the elaborate canals, in the doors of abandoned pumping stations? See Mulholland's statue smashed by vandals and the Los Angeles Department of Water and Power building empty, the temple of a cult whose gods failed? I wouldn't bet against it: not against the weight of history, the inexorability of entropy and the eternal, inescapable desert.

"Myths are things that never were, but always are," the poet-philosopher Salustius wrote. My journeys across the hidden west have been like that. Drive the back roads till they end; follow the trails till they run out . . . and then you keep going. The deeper you go into the back country, the further back in time you go. The things you find have the power of things that have endured a long, long time: pueblo, canyon, sacred mountain, splinter of an Ice Age sea; an eagle's nest built out of 6,000-year-old sticks the color of old rubbed silver. The door to that ancient, magic America is guarded by a blind Indian flute player; the maps were in the Mayan codices the Spanish burned. But if you walk long enough and hard enough, you'll find your way there in the end.

There are legends among dying peoples such as the Yokuts, the Yupik, the Hazrats, the Khampas, and other strange folk who live in the cobalt-blue country where the snows lie head-high the year round, and the ginseng roots stab the black diamond ground like forked daggers, and the sky shakes and hisses like a blanket loaded with static . . .

You place the tall bone-covered hat on your head just so, and whisper the long, convoluted incantations just so . . . And then you rise, slowly at first, up through the smokehole, out into the bright night sky. Clouds drop from your hands like icy handkerchiefs. You tear through the ultraviolet shrouds of oxygen, soaring toward the Land of the Dead, where you must go to be reborn.

Flying out of LA International at night is a lot like that. The city falls away beneath your wing, a frail skeleton of fires: El Pueblo de Nuestra Señora la Reina de Los Angeles de Porciuncula.

Even here there is so much darkness! A cold black hand (the

Santa Monica Mountains, the Hollywood Hills, the San Ga-
briels) reaches right into the heart of the city. To the west the
whole wild Pacific, a quarter of the planet, rolls away into pitch
blackness; sea lions yelp their lonely atonal songs in the Santa
Catalina Channel at the city's edge. To the east the Sierra
Nevada is already a ghostly hump of starlit snow as you rise;
and beyond is the Great Basin.

Nothing at all is known here. Mystery abides. According to
the newspaper in my lap, a Sasquatch, an American ape-man,
was sighted out in those long deserts a few miles north of Las
Vegas on an atomic test site two days ago: "a reliable infor-
mant"—a test-range employee—saw the creature at dusk, a
hairy demi-man loping away across the desert.

Darkness and wildness are everywhere, most of all in our
hearts, as we leave Cibola behind, bound across the ancient,
ghost-ridden earth.